ALSO BY RAY RAPHAEL

An Everyday History of Somewhere

THIS IS A BORZOI BOOK, PUBLISHED IN NEW YORK BY ALFRED A. KNOPF.

EDGES

EDGES

Backcountry Lives in America Today
on the Borderlands
Between the Old Ways and the New

by Ray Raphael

ALFRED A. KNOPF

New York · 1976

THIS IS A BORZOI BOOK
PUBLISHED BY ALFRED A. KNOPF, INC.

A portion of the chapter "Backcountry Economics" first appeared in *Harper's* Magazine as "Back Country Economics."

Grateful acknowledgment is made to Harper & Row, Publishers, for permission to reprint a paragraph from *Horseman, Pass By (Hud)* by Larry McMurtry.

LIBRARY OF CONGRESS CATALOGING IN PUBLICATION DATA
Raphael, Ray.
Edges: backcountry lives in America today on the borderlands between the old ways and the new.
1. California—Rural conditions.
2. Urbanization—California I. Title.
HN79.C2R36   1976   301.35'0973   75-36791
ISBN 0-394-49990-5

Manufactured in the United States of America

First Edition

For Marie

Contents

Introduction: Rounding Off the Edges   3

Part One
THE COUNTRYSIDE

1. Ranch and Timber Land   19
2. Backcountry Economics   27

Part Two
TREADING TIME IN TOWN

3. Company Town   43
4. A Victorian Village in Old Cream City   54
5. Summer Festivals:
   Rodeo, Fair, and Wildwood Days   64

Part Three
OLD FOLKS

6. The Death and Life of Old Glen Strawn   91
7. Mayme Between Two Worlds   105
8. The Last Great Days of the Vance Hotel   116

Part Four
YOUNG FOLKS

9. Scraping By   127
10. No Place Like Home   145

Contents

Part Five
THREATS TO THE EDGES:
RECREATION AND DEVELOPMENT

11. The City That Is Not 163

12. Grapes at 70 m.p.h. 173

13. Congestion in the Redwoods 184

14. Damning the Dams 194

Part Six
POSSIBILITIES

15. In This Day and Age 211

Introduction

Rounding Off the Edges

FOUR OUT OF EVERY FIVE people in the United States live in urban or suburban environments—and many of those who don't might as well. Television brings the message of mainstream American culture home to the folks left back on the farm, while automotive transportation makes the goods and services of the modern world accessible in even the most isolated areas. The neonized auto rows of our small towns are practically indistinguishable from each other; the merchandise sold in their stores is the same as that which is sold three thousand miles away. No matter how seemingly remote, we are all plugged in to a complex network of chain stores, distributors, and manufacturers that determines the fabric of our material world.

People, as a general rule, do not wish to be left behind. The glitter of city lights, with its suggestion of high times and easy living, has had an undeniable appeal for rural Americans. "I remember when I was about nineteen," says Jesse in Larry Mc-Murtry's *Hud*. "I had been on my own, and I had to go back and start helpin' Dad. We had a cotton patch in Throckmorton County, right next to the highway that ran in to Fort Worth an' Dallas and no tellin' where-all. I spent all my time following a couple of work mules around the field, and all day long folks would whiz by in their cars, going places I wanted to go. Don't think I wouldn't a given that whole run-down piece a land to a jumped in one of them cars and gone whizzing by some other pore bastard that had to work."

For all its retrospective romantic appeal, old-time life on the farm was rough. Every morning before dawn, the chickens had to be fed and the cows couldn't be left unmilked. There were no vacations with pay from the daily chores, no sick leave if you were hung over from the night before, and no welfare check to see you through if the crops failed to mature. Life hinged on a precarious balance, and it didn't take much to tip the scales against you: a fire or storm, a harvest that was never reaped, or perhaps someone else (it might be the bank) who wanted your land.

One by one the farms fell. From a Jeffersonian nation of independent farmers, we have become a society of wage earners in an industrialized world. The members of several younger generations, rather than pledging themselves to an unending life of toil on the farm, have as often as not sought alternative means of support. They have flocked to the towns and the cities, selling their labor to whoever might put it to use.

But what of those who were left behind, the people who, for one reason or another, did not become part of the march to the urbanized centers: old folks too set in their ways to change, young folks too dull (or perhaps too smart) to join the migration of their peers away from their own home towns? These I call the people of the Edges—those on the periphery of modern society who are not yet enveloped by the Metropolis. They hold one foot in the present, but the other foot is elsewhere: perhaps it is in the past—or somewhere outside of time.

Throughout rural America, towns that once were are no more. Rural counties experience a loss in population while the rest of the nation is booming. Old stores are boarded up, former farms abandoned. Once-tended orchards have been left to their own devices, and are melting back into the native landscapes. Such places, too, I call the Edges—the nooks and crannies of a countryside rich with human experience that is all but forgotten today.

4

Edges: people and places that don't quite fit, anomalies of our metropolitan times.

Many of the most interesting things, say the biologists, happen on the Edges—on the interface between the woods and the fields, the land and the sea. There, living organisms encounter dynamic conditions that give rise to untold variety. Scientific studies of bird populations reveal that "forest edge" species are generally more abundant than those which confine their territory to the interior of the forest. The intertidal zone, meanwhile, that thin ribbon which separates the land from the sea, supports a plurality of life uniquely adapted to both air and water. When the tide is high, the flora and fauna of the beaches and tide pools may provide nourishment for fish; when the tide is low, land-bound mammals such as raccoons will claim the zone as their own by feasting on the intertidal creatures. Such ecotones—areas of transition between ecological communities— owe their existence to neighboring environments, yet they seem also to create a world in themselves:

Various kinds of plants and animals not occurring, or relatively rare, in the bordering communities may become abundant in the ecotone. Shrubs typically grow in profusion at the forest edge and harbor a distinct fauna. At the margin of a pond willows and cattails thrive in the transition between land and water, and here are found such animals as turtles, frogs, herons, red-winged blackbirds, muskrats, and a host of invertebrates that are entirely absent or much less abundant in the center of the pond or in the terrain far removed from the water. . . . As a rule the ecotone contains more species and often a denser population than either of the neighboring communities, and this generality is known as the *principle of edges*. The greater variety of plants in the ecotone provides more cover and food, and thus a greater number of animals can be supported.[1]

Variety, perhaps, but there is tension as well. The flora of the meadows, as they approach the woodlands, find themselves coping with increasingly unfavorable physical conditions: the

[1] George L. Clarke, *Elements of Ecology* (New York, 1954), p. 412.

sunlight they need might be lacking, and the soil no longer feels right. There is also the problem of competition with alien species of trees and shrubs. The Edges, in short, might abound with life, but each living form must fight for its own.

The ecotones of human experience—the boundaries where two cultures meet—are similarly enriched with variety but fraught with tension. Neighboring societies often seek contact through trade, but sometimes they fight each other instead. In the pluralistic world of today, differing ethnic groups and communities have learned to exist side by side, although not always with the greatest of ease. American blacks have been systematically oppressed by whites, who have simultaneously adopted elements of black culture with great fervor. European immigrants, once foreigners, have themselves helped determine the texture of mainstream society. Indeed, does not all of American culture have its genesis in the intersection of varying peoples from around the world? Is not the American melting pot an example par excellence of what can happen in the ecotones of human communities?

It is here, however, that our biological analogy breaks down, for differing peoples, unlike separate species of flora and fauna, can be made to become the same. If American society were a biological community, we would still hear scores of different languages as we crossed from one neighborhood to the next; we would still see customs and costumes that have long since disappeared from the fabric of our daily lives. Plants in an ecotone might have to fight for survival, but if they succeed they will at least remain intact. Human culture, however, is more subject to change, and the changes that come can be swift. It takes but a generation to forget one's native tongue, and less than that to pick up the uniform, manipulated language of the mass media. Instead of regionalized cooking, we now find hamburgers and french fries wherever we go; where once we had local dialects, we now talk more and more like the people we see on TV. Will there be any ethnic communities left in fifty or a hundred years? Will the standardized culture by then have consumed us all?

Fortunately, standardization is not a one-way process. Fearful of a Brave New World, Americans are beginning to demonstrate a renewed interest in ethnic and cultural identities. In the ten years since the words "black power" awakened the nation to the reality that some people did not *want* to be included in a happily integrated State of Nowhere, a host of other groups have come to the fore claiming that they too do not wish to be subsumed by mass culture, that they too wish to have their individual identities preserved. Chicanos, Chinese, and Indians; old people, students, and even kids—the word is out to be proud of who you are, to cherish instead of to deny the particular culture to which you belong.

And now to these groups I would add yet another: rural folk, plain and simple Americans who still live close to the land, who don't care to put on airs, who prefer to remain the way they are. These, again, are the people of the Edges, those caught on the interface between a traditional country way of life and the forces of modernization that threaten to annihilate it. Their kinship ties are strong, their feeling for their homes profound—yet these very virtues, once the backbone of traditional American culture, are now seen as obsolete in a society constantly on the move. The average length of residency in a single abode for a city dweller today is only four years; the occupation of sons and daughters is usually not the same as that of their folks. In metropolitan circles there is little sense of a unified place—one's home, one's ranch, one's own home town—or of a continuity in time. People act more and more as their own free agents, neither bound by familial obligations nor trapped by a heritage of antiquated traditions and norms. The past is whisked away in the eagerness to get on with the business of the future.

Yet the past is not so easily forgotten. Life itself hinges precariously on the ever-changing interface between the past and the present, the present and the future. Each and every moment is a time of transition. The accelerated rate of change in our modern world serves only to accentuate these most disturbing realities: the past is lost forever, while the future remains uncertain. In vain we turn to nostalgia, to the glorification of the not too distant culture of yesterday. We would like to hold on to something secure—whatever that may be. And since rural life is largely a thing of the past, we covet its remnants as symbols of more peaceful times: old lamps and cookstoves, wicker chairs and rockers, granny dresses and overalls have thus become fashionable acquisitions within cosmopolitan circles.

With time flying faster than ever and the space-age future quick upon us, we have suddenly awakened to the fact that our countryside itself might soon be lost for good. Conservation of land and resources has become the *cause célèbre* of our time. After centuries of gazing at infinite horizons, we are now aware that our planet is indeed quite finite. And so the forgotten countryside has once again taken on meaning as the last frontier of natural beauty, a reminder to the folks of the Metropolis that Mother Nature still exists.

Yet with all the push toward conservation of the land, and with all those country-culture antiques meticulously preserved in suburban homes, there is curiously little attention paid to the actual people who still inhabit the Edges. At best, they are seen as upstate conservatives, obstacles to progressive (and often conservationist) movements. Our ecological consciousness has sensitized us to "endangered species," but have we extended that consciousness to "endangered cultures," to the lives and lifestyles of the people of the Edges? Indeed, human beings are part and parcel of the "natural" environment. When we bemoan the loss of wildlife due to the engineered development of natural areas, we ought also to pay some attention to the social consequences of that development, to the human ecology of the backcountry being forced, willy-nilly, into the Now Generation.

While the developers and the conservationists engage in battle over how best to use the landscape, the people of the Edges, the ones who still live close to the earth, have their own perspective on the situation. They seek neither parks nor developments—they only want their ranches to remain intact. They don't like subdivisions for recreational homes—those will only raise their taxes and drive them from their land. Nor do they seek additional wilderness areas which deprive their local communities of the harvesting of natural resources. In their struggle for survival, the people of the Edges—the still backwaters of the countryside—wish simply to be left alone.

The threat to the last remnants of nonurbanized America

stems directly from the rapid shrinkage of space in recent times. Isolation is no longer a safeguard. Television waves serve as an instant denial of distance, and motorized transportation as a denial that is almost as quick. Our globe has become so small that no piece of land, whether it is productive or not, can afford to be ignored. The backcountry which has harbored the stubborn holdouts of rural living through most of the twentieth century is now desired as a playground to service the overcrowded cities. Second-home developments, artificial lakes, highways into no-where—these are the demands being placed on the countryside, demands which amount to a notice of eviction for the people of the Edges.

Land, that priceless resource, has taken on value precisely because it is scarce, and the backcountry folks are suddenly dis-covering that their old homesteads have become precious pieces of real estate. At first it might seem a blessing, but in reality it is not: the only way they can take advantage of their new-found asset is to sell out. Otherwise, they are burdened with steadily increasing taxes and harassed by forces representing the people of plenty: the investors who would develop their land, the tim-ber companies that would log it, the government agencies that would conserve it.

The people of the Edges are scared. Big business controls the money, big agriculture controls the land, big government con-trols the laws. In a thousand different ways, the bureaucracy has already extended its unwanted arms into their lives. A rancher named Fred Wolf, for instance, suddenly discovers that he is no longer allowed to do what he's done all along:

It's getting so you can't hardly even butcher your own livestock and sell it. These butchers, and what have you, they say it's gotta be cut and killed and federal inspected. Years back, I butchered fifty, sixty lambs a year. Well, I butchered five this year and I got a tip that I better lay off, and I quit. Before, if you wanted a couple of lambs, I sold to you, and I had a business built up. But now I gotta sell live through the auction.

Then there's the building inspectors, the health inspectors, the tax men, the various commissioners for this and that, and the banks and the bill collectors and . . . The message is clear:

you've got to do things thus and so, and if you don't—well, we have the power to close you down.

My home is on the Edges, in the backhills of northwestern California generally considered too rugged and inhospitable for large-scale agriculture. The area is not heavily populated: my congressional district, if we can use that as a measure, stretches for some three hundred miles. I live without the blessings of electricity, telephone, or television; I do so of necessity, since the electric and telephone lines come to an end five miles away. The nearest town, ten miles from my home, did not have electricity until 1950. There is one road into town (paved) and one road out of it (dirt). Downtown—the general store and post office—is guarded through the night by a single street light and a neon sign advertising the beer which sometimes is—and sometimes is not—available within the store.

Although remote, the countryside here has not always been neglected. Indians once thrived on acorns, salmon, and deer; homesteaders scraped together a modest living in the small, isolated valleys. The heavily wooded hillsides were stripped first of their tan oak trees (the bark was used in tanning leather); then of their redwood and Douglas fir. But the periodic population booms created by work in the woods were short-lived: once the tan bark was superseded by synthetic processes, and once the first-growth stands of timber were exhausted, many of the folks who had made their living here moved on.

But some stayed. An occasional rancher who did not sell out, former loggers who have grown old with their land—these are my neighbors, the people of the Edges who serve as the inspiration for this book. As a rule, they are a hard and crusty lot, often lacking the style, manners, and social graces that would place them in good stead in uptown society. They know how to wield an ax and milk a cow, but they would make poor clerical workers, nor would they take well to mechanized routines. In their everyday habits they straddle two worlds: they can their own catsup and buy mustard at the store, they drink dandelion wine and Miller's beer.

Today, these backhill natives are joined by a new group of country folk, young émigrés from the city seeking a life less removed from basic necessity and more closely linked with natural forces. Like their old-time mentors, the young people cultivate gardens, raise animals, and home-can much of their food. Having self-consciously adopted agrarian ways, these converts to the Edges now volunteer to take up the torch of a lifestyle which the old-timers had all but given up for a thing of the past.

Yet the coastal hills of California are attracting the attention of other interests as well. "The place is ripe for development," say the investors and real estate brokers whose business it is to provide land for those who can afford it. Each year the developments creep further up the coast, extending outward from the metropolitan areas to the south. As the freeways make car travel quicker, as city folk gain more leisure time, and as the environmental quality of the cities themselves continues to deteriorate, the market for vacation homes and recreational land mushrooms. Maybe you can't grow crops, maybe the timber is gone—but let there be no doubt about it: land in the backcountry (indeed, land almost *anywhere*) will not long be neglected.

What is happening here is happening throughout America. The New England countryside, Appalachian foothills, Rocky Mountain wastelands, painted deserts of the Southwest—places which were formerly deemed virtually worthless from an economic point of view—are suddenly in demand. The intensified drive for land presents a challenge to the natural environment, and to the human environment as well. The people who live in these backcountry areas have, whether consciously or not, based their manner of living largely around the very absence of large-scale development and technology. They have grown accustomed to population declines—and all of a sudden the population threatens to skyrocket beyond all previous levels. The newcomers arrive from a different world, bringing with them a whole new set of interests and values. In a thousand different ways, the people and places of the Edges are disrupted, threatened, changed into what they have never been.

For many areas of the country, the challenge is not a new

one. The midwestern bread basket, California salad bowl, Wisconsin dairy land—the fertile farm lands have long since been taken over by large-scale, highly technological corporations. There, the family farm is a creature of the distant past. In California, for instance, two thirds of the farm land is taken up by one twentieth of the farms, and these giant plantations are most certainly not of the "Ma and Pa" variety. Agribusiness, like any other industry, functions exclusively with machines and hired labor. The poorly paid workers in the fields might not be part of the American mainstream, but neither are they the last remnants of a traditional agrarian lifestyle.

Insofar as the Edges are economically depressed (which, indeed, they are), people are often forced into a lower standard of living than they would like. Wearing overalls and heating with wood might be matters of style and convenience, aspects of a mode of life which the people of the Edges have consciously chosen, but nobody chooses to be so poor that they cannot afford decent medical care and three square meals a day—or a vacation now and then. Yet many of the folks on the Edges *are* that poor, and thus economics is a gut-level issue which must be tackled head on. How can people's financial condition be improved without sacrificing those more amorphous considerations having to do with the "quality of life"? How can the Edges be economically developed without serious side effects to the physical and social environments? These are questions which cannot be ignored.

Many of the problems faced by the people of the Edges are echoed throughout our society. In the hearts of our largest cities, old folks are ignored and neglected, left to live out their days in a subhuman world. In the city as well as the country there is a scarcity of decent housing, yet the construction industry still pushes for restrictive regulations which inhibit individuals from doing the work themselves. And in the name of economic progress, ridiculous projects and developments are undertaken anywhere and everywhere to give artificial props to a sagging economy. Indeed, the Edges are a part of our world; the problems they face are our own. In the isolated setting of the countryside, however, we may be able to perceive our social problems from a clearer perspective. In the particular analysis of a given environment, the universal principles which apply to us all might be revealed; in the microcosm of my own particular Edges, I have experienced, and hope to convey, some insights into the social and ecological dynamics of our times.

This book consists of a series of portraits in which the people and places of the Edges are allowed to speak for themselves. Within each subject the interplay of opposites is busily at work: old and new, city and country, power and powerlessness, standardization and local variation, individuality and bureaucracy. This polarity generates an atmosphere of electric excitement in which nothing is certain, everything is tenuous. For every trend in one direction, there are other tendencies that lead the opposite way. Within each essay the whole story of the Edges should be revealed, for the emphasis is always on that most fragile yet stimulating interface between past and present, present and future.

I start with the setting: the countryside and small towns which cling precariously to rural traditions. With nostalgia now a national fad, the fashion today is to regard such places as quaint, harmless holdovers from the past. But that is not my perception. From the vibrating power lines over peaceful pastures to the dune buggies which have superseded horses on the merry-go-round at the rodeo, what I see are contradictory forces pulling in several directions at once. The ranch country would like to resist change, but it cannot resist the temptation for profitable business ventures in the modern-day world. The towns would glorify their rural traditions while simultaneously reaching eagerly for a commercial economy suited to the twentieth century. Town and country alike, the places of the Edges are at a crossroads, for they, like the Metropolis they serve, are more subject to change now than ever before.

From the places, I move to the people themselves: the old folks who have had to adjust their country ways to a city-dominated world—and the young folks from the cities who are trying to do the reverse. Here again, I offer a series of portraits of people who are coping with contradictory social forces. Glen, at the time of his death, is made into something he is not;

Mayme, both Indian and Christian, has integrated opposing social traditions into the framework of a single life. The often ironic complexities of character are reflections of distinct cultures which have come to meet at the Edges. The young pioneers carry these ironies to the extreme: their re-creation of the past is made into a wave of the future; in the name of tradition they challenge the established society under which they were reared; their very presence has altered the fabric of the rural life which they seek as their own.

In the final section I talk of the specific threats to the people and places of the Edges—the dams, highways, parks, and developments which could ultimately consume and annihilate their separate modes of existence. But here again, the forces lead both ways: the developments don't always succeed, and the dams don't always get built.

Since the development of the countryside is generally undertaken in the name of economic necessity, I conclude by offering some alternative solutions to the economic woes of depressed, depleted areas. My suggestions are gleaned from personal experiences with life on the Edges and from some of the examples set by the people who appear in this book. I try to show that economics and ecology don't always have to be at odds with each other, that human occupation of the earth does not of necessity mean exploitation of the natural world. The lesson to be learned from the example of the Edges is one of proper utilization of diminishing resources. And on an individual level, the people of the Edges can offer us a model for productive, nonwasteful living which runs counter to the general trend of our consumer-oriented economy.

Since the Edges I speak of are my own, it would be safe to conclude that I have a vested interest in how it all comes down in the end. I experience the conflicts and tensions of the Edges on a firsthand basis: it seems that I am constantly going to meetings concerning what some agency or other proposes to do with the land on which I live. Rather than attempt to adopt the pseudo objectivity expected of most reporters, I have chosen to make my feelings clear, hoping thereby to arrive at a level of insight and analysis not possible when events are perceived only from the outside. I thus see my own participation as a welcomed, and perhaps necessary, adjunct to the type of involved reportage in which personal sensitivity and depth of feeling are aspired to rather than shunned.

The interplay of opposing forces has created an unstable environment of dynamic action here in the backcountry of northern California. There is still a plurality of cultural norms, still a touch of country funk which stands in defiance of the forces of modernization which threaten to do it in. And there is still a sense of adventure: places to go and situations to experience which are not charted out in advance. But how long can it last? There are those who foresee only doom; the Edges, they say, can't possibly survive in a technological society that re-creates the world after its own image. Personally, I am not so sure. True, the backcountry will change, but it might, just *might*, change into something which still belongs to itself—and which can give a few lessons to the rest of our shrinking world.

Part One
THE COUNTRYSIDE

You can't make a living off that land.
You just can't do it any more.

—AN OLD-TIMER

---

in space, with the earth below and the sky above. Beyond the farthest ridge to the east lies the Eel River valley, whose giant redwoods are the tallest trees in the world; to the south the open range gradually gives way to a maze of cut-over brush; to the north the few square miles of lowlands surrounding Humboldt Bay contain more than half the population of the entire county; and to the west, stretching out to an infinite horizon, lies the Pacific Ocean, bearer of summer fogs, winter storms, and moderate temperatures throughout the year. This is my world: the fields, forests, towns, and open seas of the North Coast of California.

If the Cape Mendocino ranch country seems naked, the Eel River valley is dressed to the hilt. Where the state parks have managed to preserve the prehistoric redwood forests, a thick canopy of vegetation covers every square inch of the earth's surface. The mammoth trunks of the trees, perfectly straight and regular, are without living limbs to the height of about one hundred feet; above that, another hundred feet of branches keep all but a flickering of sunlight from reaching the forest floor. The dense shade beneath is carpeted with a soft coating of fallen branchlets and—except where it has been purposely cleared—a lush covering of ferns, vines, and bushes. It has been said before, but I'll say it again: if ever a twentieth-century person hopes to catch a glimpse of the forest primeval, this is surely the place.

But the virgin redwood forests which once stretched continuously for hundreds of miles have been reduced to a mere fraction of their former size. The majority of trees in the majority of locations have long since disappeared, having been transformed into the Victorian houses of San Francisco and other structures for humans in other cities and towns across the country. Where the logging was done long ago, second-growth forests, decidedly smaller imitations of their predecessors, are now themselves being harvested; where the logging has been only recent, slender new shoots form rings around the stumps of the former giants and a host of sun-loving bushes and weeds invade the once shady terrain. The virgin Redwood Wonderland, which attracts millions of awestruck tourists to the California North, thus consists for the most part of only a few thin ribbons of trees which line the highway; the dominant reality of the rest of the landscape is one of periodic growth and destruction, since the production and harvesting of timber afford the local human inhabitants their primary source of livelihood.

The backhills to the south of Cape Mendocino are noted neither for their redwoods nor for their expanse of grazing land. Indeed, they have (or had) a little of both, as well as a lot of mixed forests of oak and Douglas fir. But the forests have been harvested twice—once for the oaks and their tannic acids, once for the lumber provided by the fir and the redwoods—and the hillsides today consist primarily of ten-, twenty-, and thirty-year-old scrub. There is some ranch land scattered about, but this is not always used for grazing. Instead, much of the countryside has been chopped by developers into second-home communities, set aside by the government for purposes of recreation, or recycled by young people into modern versions of old-time homesteads. Despite such civilizing influences, however, the countryside still appears untamed: the wild animals of the forest are more frequent than domesticated livestock, the terrain is more rugged than the open hillsides up on the Cape, and the people themselves tend to be more of a rough-and-tumble lot.

The Humboldt Bay region, on the other hand, affords the North Coast its closest approximation of a Metropolis. Eureka, the county seat, boasts of a population of some thirty thousand modern-day souls. The style of life there is basically the same as in any other medium-sized town or small city in America: people live in apartments or individual houses with yards but no real land; they go to work on jobs which are determined more by the clock than the weather; they shop for their food and other necessities at the store and are provided with heat, light, and power by the local utility company. Much of the landscape is dominated by the automobile and its accessories: highways, roads, parking lots, driveways, drive-ins, gas stations, and the rest. Yet Eureka is not really that large, and it isn't far to where the prize dairy herds of the silt-laden Eel River delta seem to take over from the cars.

Finally, to the west, there is the ocean, home of numerous fish, sea mammals, crustaceans, mollusks—but scarcely any people. Even to us landlubbers, however, the proximity of the ocean is important: it determines our weather and thus plays a crucial role in the selection of our natural and agricultural resources; it provides us with a seemingly (although not truly) fathomless source of food; it guarantees us one last frontier upon which other human beings are not likely to settle. Cape Mendocino is the westernmost extension of California, and, Americans that we are, we cannot help but attach some significance to the fact that we are at the very end of our westward leanings, the last human outposts between the land and the sea. We find ourselves, quite literally, on the Edges of America.

Western civilization has inhabited, and dominated, the California North Coast for scarcely over a century, yet many settlements and towns which so recently appeared on the landscape have already been abandoned, lost, and forgotten. Cape Mendocino's Capetown, for instance, had a population of 150 in 1909; today the town no longer exists. Then, there was a hotel with fifteen bedrooms and complete dining facilities, a general store, a post office, a livery stable, a blacksmith's shop, a cooper's shop, a school with three dozen children, and a "town hall" for dances and celebrations; now, the entire town is subsumed by a single ranch. "When they had all the children in school," says Helen Branstetter, who runs the Capetown ranch with her husband, Prescott, "it was all dairies in through here. They were hundred-cow dairies, and of course they were milked by hand. And the men that milked the cows had families and they lived all over these hills. Then the children would ride their horses down to school here. So this was really quite a community."

Whatever happened to Capetown and its dairies? How does a farming town disappear so quickly? "They couldn't sell the butter because of the inspections and things like that," says Prescott Branstetter. "The barns were old and the inspection laws came along and condemned them, even just to milk in. And with the price of labor it was hard to get help. The cost of transportation out here was something else, too. All the involvements which go with the dairy business—they're having a hard enough time now down in the valley, right next to the creameries."

Then there was the automobile. Capetown had been the midway point between Petrolia and Ferndale, each fifteen miles away. Back in the old days the stage would have to stop overnight, while private travelers would at least stop over for lunch. The herdsmen, meanwhile, would base themselves in Capetown during the four-day cattle drive from one town to the next. But the car, of course, changed all that, for what was a day's journey then is now done in an hour. Capetown, like midway spots everywhere, was simply whisked off the map.

Capetown, Ettersburg, Upper Bear River—the countryside here is dotted with towns which no longer exist. In Upper Bear River, Bob and Sid Morrison still live on the land that their grandfather settled in 1856. They used to have a school of their own, but now the place is deserted—except, of course, for the stock. "Most of this country is owned by the Russ Company," explains seventy-six-year-old Sid, "and they don't have any men on the ranches any more. They just more or less let them run themselves. That's to cut down on the overhead. The price of wages is so high now that it's just not in the cards to have a man on the ranch. It's cheaper to lose a few head of stock than it is to hire a man. And the same thing is true down in the valley. Used to be if a man had twenty acres he could raise a family and educate 'em there. Now twenty acres won't support one person. The expenses are so great, and the income is so low on it. Comparatively. There are some small dairies in there, but now they are combining. They're going into larger dairies and market milk things now. So that's the way the thing is going all over the country, so far as I can see. You've got to expand or get out."

"It's getting larger all the time and always has," adds Johnnie Chambers, a Petrolia rancher who is also descended from the first white settlers. "Used to be that a ranch that would run a hundred head of cows, four or five hundred head of sheep, would support a family. That isn't true any more. Now they figure if you can't run three hundred head of cows you can't make a living off of it. So now these ranches have mostly got larger, or else they've sold off and split up. Of course, you look back and see our forefathers came in and homesteaded this country on small pieces like that. But eventually they starved to death on it, they had to sell out. This country here, you go back in the hills and find old homesteads all through it. Even the remains of old cabins where they used to make a living, raise their family on a corn patch and everything else."

While the trend toward consolidation was creating bigger ranches run by fewer people, the forests, on their part, were becoming steadily smaller. "California will for centuries have virgin forests, perhaps to the end of Time!" proclaimed an early visitor to the Redwood Empire. But the European Americans wasted little time in tearing these forests down. "At every available point for shipment stands a saw mill turning trees to lumber, furnishing employment for labor and investment for capital," boasted an early historian. At first it was horse and bull teams, then steam donkeys, and finally Caterpillars and trucks—as the technology advanced, logging operations spread from the accessible valleys to the remote and rugged backhill terrain. And as each particular area was harvested, logging camps and small towns quickly arose, only to be abandoned as soon as the trees were gone. Today, all the small mills have closed down, leaving only the giant companies to harvest the second-growth forests.

The landscape has been dominated by timber and ranching, but loggers and ranchers aren't the only human creatures to be found on this space on earth. There are merchants and professionals to service the countryfolk, rangers to tend to the parks, fishermen to seek food and a livelihood from the nearby Pacific. Then there are those who run the drive-through trees and curio shops and motels, the proprietors of the forest who manage to leave the trees standing while exploiting them nonetheless. In one way or another, the people who live here have managed to scrape together a living, to adapt to the changing times.

But many of the former residents have been forced to move on. In the 1960's, while the rest of the state was booming and California was becoming the most populous state in the nation, the population of the North Coast counties substantially decreased. With fewer trees to cut and fewer jobs on the open range, the economy declined along with the population. What could a young person do to make his way in the world? What opportunities were left for the young folks here?

John, age nineteen, is just out of high school. He has moved out on his own, learned to cook and do his wash at the laundromat, and has been fortunate enough to find a job in the woods setting choke (fastening logs to the rig that will take them out of the forest). In his first month of work he made a thousand dollars—more money than he had ever seen at one time. "Don't ask me where a nickel of it is," he says proudly, " 'cause I couldn't tell you." He has purchased eight new sports jackets and now dresses in style. Ambitious, he is filled with ideas about how he will make his fortune. He has heard that firewood sells for a hundred twenty-five dollars a cord down in L.A. and is preparing to set up a little sideline of his own. But firewood, for the Los Angeleans, has to look just right. Random sizes, shapes, and species of wood will simply never do—especially at the premium price they are willing to pay. Rather than salvage fallen logs, as is the general practice here in the backcountry, John has therefore resolved to cut down live trees. If John's mill job falls through, as well it might, his firewood sideline might become his vocation. A modern-day logger, he seeks new ways to turn his home-town forests into personal profit. He is a wave of the future, an example of what probably lies ahead for many of these small-town boys and second-growth woods.

Dan, on the other hand, has a somewhat different attitude toward his future. Like John, he has just moved out on his own and has managed to find work as a hired hand on a neighbor's ranch. His father runs a small ranch nearby, but there's not enough there for the two of them and Dan would like to get a place of his own. "But I don't see how I can," he concedes. "They cost a lot of money, and nobody wants to sell out anyway. But whether I have my own place or not, I just want to work on a ranch. Even if I can't keep my job over here, I'll get a job somewhere else. Just so it's on a ranch. Ranching is something that gets bred into you. It's hard ever to get rid of it. Ranching is all I've ever known."

At a time of great social mobility, when one generation is scarcely recognizable by the next, it is surprising to see any young people at all who, like Dan, still take after their folks, hoping only to do what has always been done. But traditionalism is strong in the Cape Mendocino ranch country, even if it is threatened daily. The Chamberses, the Branstetters, the Morrisons—they all date back to the first white settlers, and they all have children who are ready and willing to carry on the line. "As far as this ranching business is concerned," says Bob Morrison, "it's a way of life. It's something I've always done. I've been on this ranch or up at the next place all *my* life, my father was here all *his* life, and my grandfather was the first white man in this country. So we've been here all this time. We like it. We like the way we live. I guess that's about all you can say for it. In all this time I been around this place mechanics have been making more money than I have, probably. Still, I keep my head above water all right. We live pretty well, and we like what we're doing, so I guess that's why we're still here. We could sell the damn place out at the inflated value of land for an awful lot of money, but I don't want to do that. I got enough to get by, and I don't know what I'd do with money. The rewards of the thing are the life that you live as much as the money you make."

Here in the person of Bob Morrison is rural America, still struggling to remain intact. He and young Dan speak for the people of the Edges who would resist the forces of consolidation and/or development which threaten their land and their lifestyle. But there are others who would rather swim with the tide, making their money however they might. Yes, money—for it is in the name of economics that changes are born. The ranch and timber land here, like the countryside anywhere, cannot fully be understood without reference to that all-pervasive reality: people must manage a livelihood somehow, and the occupations they choose are bound to affect the land upon which they live.

2

Backcountry Economics

THE FIRST TIME I ever drove past Petrolia's general store, I noticed a mimeographed sheet of paper dangling from the wall on the porch. It was an announcement for an important meeting of all local citizens to see what they could do about the encroachment of the federal government into their world. At issue were the newly created Redwood National Park and the Bureau of Land Management's King Range National Conservation Area. What, I wondered, do these people have against preserving the environment?

A few miles farther south, near another small settlement called Honeydew, I smelled smoke. As I drove on I could see the charred hillsides still smoldering, a motley array of scrubby snags rising out of the debris like ancient ruins. I found a Forest Ranger sitting calmly in his car and asked him if everything was under control. It always had been, he said. The people set it themselves. His job was simply to sit and watch, just in case. When you play with fire, he said, sometimes you burn your fingers.

Don't these people, I asked him, care about the environment? How could they do such a thing?

They did it, he said, to clear the land for ranching. It had just been logged and wasn't much good for anything the way it was. They did it all the time. Even the more established ranchers burned their fields to facilitate the growth of next year's grass.

I asked him about the notice I had seen outside the store in Petrolia. Why did the local people oppose the parks?

Jobs, he said. If they don't cut down the trees, people are out of work. And that's the only kind of work they can get up here.

The root of it all, in a word, was economic necessity. The people had to make a living somehow. If that meant the trees had to be cut, then who's to tell them they couldn't? If that meant the land had to be burned, then who's to tell them they shouldn't?

I thought of the squirrels and rabbits trapped in the fire. And baby birds. But such concerns are a luxury reserved for those who have already solved their own struggle for survival. How strange that so much of the recent conservationist push comes from city dwellers, from people who in their daily lives are totally out of contact with the land, while the country folk, who would appear to live closer to nature, so often oppose the conservationists. But the urbanites make their living elsewhere, in offices and shops and factories far away from the forests. When they come to the country, they come to play. The local people are here to work. "If things keep a-goin' the way they are," complains Capetown rancher Prescott Branstetter, "won't be long before the Bureau of Land Management will take all this land and make a playground for the rest of the country. That's what we're disturbed about in our particular area because none of us want to have our ranches taken away from us, even though they pay us for it. Just so everybody can have access to a play-ground of the world. Pretty soon they'll all be playing and there'll be no production to feed the people that's half starving to death now." With one man's playground being another man's workshop, is it any wonder that conflicts develop over how best to use the land?

The economic pressures faced by country folk are seldom taken into consideration by ecologically concerned citizens. We want to preserve the environment, but we tend to be somewhat naïve in our understanding of the economic dynamics that often lead to destructive land-use practices. The people of the Edges, however, know these dynamics well: they live with them day by day. Here, in brief, are some of the unfortunate realities that lie behind the continuing rape of the countryside.

TIMBER

Let's say you're the proud owner of one of the few remaining stands of virgin redwood or Douglas fir. Perhaps you acquired the land years ago and it's fully paid off. But your taxes are not. The assessed valuation of your land includes the market value of your trees, each one of which is worth hundreds, even thousands, of dollars. Thus each year you are taxed anew on your unused timber. If you own forty, twenty, or even just ten acres of virgin forest, your annual tax bill will be several thousand dollars. Unless you are independently wealthy, you are left with only one reasonable alternative: cut your trees. And after you cut them, the California State Constitution guarantees you will not face another timber tax for forty years, while the county assessor can extend this period even longer. You are left with tens of thousands of dollars in immediate cash and virtually no taxes for the rest of your lifetime. The decision to cut or not to cut is hardly a decision at all—it has already been made for you.

Or perhaps your forest is not a virgin one but was logged in the early 1900's. Your trees are now growing quickly, but your forty-year immunity is over and each year your taxes are getting larger. Once again, you are tempted to harvest your trees—even though they are not really mature. A computer analysis of various California forests, assuming "complete economic rationality" on the part of the timber holders, has shown that the current taxation methods result in cutting the trees before their maximum biological productivity has been reached. Just when they are growing the fastest, economic realities dictate that the trees be cut to the ground. The computer results show that the average annual output of the forests studied could be increased by between 24 and 94 percent—if only the method of taxation would be changed.

Not all states include a timber tax as part of the property tax. Some have what is called a yield tax, in which the trees are taxed only when they are cut. From an environmental viewpoint the yield tax, which tends to dissuade rather than encourage the logging of virgin forests and the premature harvest of second-growth timber, is obviously preferable to the property tax. But local governments are hesitant to switch over to the yield tax because the revenue arrives at the tax collector's office in fits and starts rather than in a nice steady stream. A slow year in the logging industry could consequently deal a deathblow to the county budget. Where the yield tax is in effect, the tax rate is usually quite high in an attempt to compensate for this inconvenience. And thus, where the timber holders are given a choice between a property and a yield tax, as they are in Oregon, they often favor the former anyway because the percentage taken by the government in the latter seems exorbitant.

In California most of the logging companies are perfectly happy with things the way they are. Their stands of virgin timber have long since disappeared and hence are not taxed. The regrowth is exempted from taxation for forty years, shortly after which (at least in the case of redwood) the timber can again be harvested and they can enjoy another forty-year period of exemption. What is lost in biological productivity is gained in the frequency of the harvests—and in the virtual absence of taxes. The tax laws, in short, are written to promote, and even necessitate, the cutting of virgin timber and the periodic re-harvesting of the new growth. And this, of course, is precisely what the logging companies wish to do.

The large companies, furthermore, only pay about one half of the taxes that a small timber holder would pay for the same trees. This special discount is given on the basis of what is called an "evaluation factor" (it used to be called simply a "discount rate," but that term was recently dropped since it revealed rather than concealed the discrepancies). The official justification for the discount goes like this: The timber is taxed as if it were all going to be cut down in a given year, but the holdings of the big companies are so expansive that they couldn't possibly cut down all their trees at once. Hence, only a fraction of the estimated value of the timber is taxed. The reasoning seems bizarre—but that's really the way it works. Again, the tax laws are very direct in telling the small timber holder exactly what to do: harvest your trees—you'd better, because we're taxing you as if you already did.

What does all this mean for the people of the Edges? Whether they ranch or not, many of the local folks own some land, and much of the land is forested. Economic realities have told them to cut down their trees, and most have already done so. But where does that leave them now? "There's been a lot of timber sold out of this country in the last few years," says Sid Morrison. "That has given the ranchers a boost. It's brought some of 'em out of a tough spot, and others it's given quite a bit of additional money. But nearly all the private timber is gone in here now, and it won't happen again for quite some time." For those who did not have enough to get rich, the period of economic reprieve is over. "Timber is what has kept these ranches alive for the last twenty years," says Johnnie Chambers. "Now that it's gone, they're hurting."

And what do you do with land that has just been logged? It will be almost half a century before you can reap another harvest of your trees, but you don't have to wait that long to get your land back in the habit of making money. You can burn off the remaining undergrowth (the government will help you for free), sow some grass seeds, and switch over to sheep ranching. Stump ranches, as they are called, have thus sprung up all over the formerly wooded countryside.

One way or another, the idea is to make your land work for you rather than against you. Cut it, burn it, ranch it—whatever works. And if all else fails, there's always the possibility of subdivision and development.

RANCHING

Let's say you are a rancher. Maybe you have ranched all your life, or perhaps you used to be a timber holder who has since turned his land over to grass and sheep. In either case, the problem of taxes has not been solved. As new developments spring up across the nearby countryside, the assessed valuation of your land will go up. Sheep ranching is a marginal business requiring large holdings of land, and taxes can hurt. As Fred Wolf, a rancher near Ettersburg, puts it:

In 1958, for this here 700 acres, I paid 185 dollars in taxes. I ain't got a bit more now than I had then, and taxes last year [1971] was 600 dollars. They claim they don't raise the tax rates, but where they get you is they increase the assessed valuation all the time. Used to be, in this country here, you could buy 40 acres, timber and all, for 100 dollars. Now the son of a bitch is more than 100 dollars an acre.

That's not enough to do Fred in. Not yet. But the ranches all around him are being divided and sold. Land values are shooting up, doubling and tripling every few years. It's only a matter of time before Fred will be paying thousands of dollars in taxes. And that just might be enough to do him in.

Unless, of course, he can come up with other sources of revenue. Perhaps he might try adding more sheep to his flock, but then there's the danger of overgrazing and subsequent erosion. Or perhaps Fred's ranch can be used by hunters as well as sheep.

What's coming up now is these hunting clubs. If you got enough property, you can get ten guys in there and get a hundred dollars apiece. Well, a lot of 'em will pay that 'cause there ain't no other place to go. If you got ten guys, that's a thousand bucks, and you can't make a thousand bucks any easier. There's a lot of them that's doin' that, 'cause it's easy money, extry income.

Ranchers in some areas of California can now find partial tax relief by applying for classification as an "agricultural preserve" under the Williamson Open Spaces Act of 1965. The property owner must agree to restrict his land over a ten-year period to agricultural or forest uses. In turn, his assessment will be based on the potential productivity of his land rather than on its actual market value, which might be considerably higher. Thus the land's potential value for subdivision and development is not taken into consideration in the assessment, but the owner is bound by contract, under severe civil penalties, not to sell his land for purposes of speculation or development during the period in question.

The Williamson Act has already saved many a rancher from

being forced to sell out. But not all ranchers have been so fortunate. The act allows each county to decide the extent to which it wishes to implement the law, or whether it wishes to deal with it at all. And not all counties have rushed to the aid of the distressed ranchers. Insofar as the Williamson Act offers a "tax break" to one particular group, other taxpayers who would have to take up the slack have been quick to oppose it.

And even some of the ranchers themselves have been hesitant to avail themselves of the tax break offered by the Williamson Act. Ranchers often go into debt, and selling off a little land is sometimes the only way to meet the mortgage on the ranch as a whole. But selling land is precisely what the Williamson Act forbids the ranchers from doing. According to Johnnie Chambers,

Ranches are only running on borrowed money. Now there's only one way out for a rancher to ever make any money, and that's on the increase in land value, which has been going up. What we paid a hundred dollars an acre for ten years ago today is worth three hundred dollars. But the only way to realize that is to sell it. So if you get tied up in this Williamson Act, you can't sell it. It really puts you in a bind. I mean, selling some land may be your only salvation. The ranchers got a mortgage on their place, so what are they gonna do? They're gonna lose it. So maybe their best bet is to sell it, pay the mortgage off, stick the rest in their pocket, and move into something else. But if they're in the Williamson Act, they can't do this. The Williamson Act is a good deal for the bigger operations that have a lot of acreage. They can ride these kind of times out. But the little guy that's gotta meet his mortgage every year . . . if cattle and wool prices stay down like this, it's gonna fold a lot of 'em. There's no way in the world they can make it if they got a loan on their ranch, with interest.

The ranchers' economic position, it seems, is always uncertain. They know how many stock they have on the ranch, they know how many are ready to be sold, but they don't have any guarantee at all of the price that they'll fetch. "A year ago," recalls Sid Morrison, "they got good prices for their stock. Then this year they got just half that much. Sixty-five cents for calves last fall, thirty-two cents this fall, see? That's a heck of a drop.

Lambs are more nearly stable than the cattle are, but the wool market is very peculiar. Last year the price of wool went up to a dollar, a dollar thirty cents a pound. And the next day you couldn't *sell* a pound of wool. *Nobody* would make an offer on it. The bottom dropped out of it overnight. Why, I don't know. Manipulation, I'd judge."

Why, one might ask, don't the ranchers hold on to their stock until the prices go back up? "Well, the ranchers can't afford to do it," says Johnnie Chambers. "You can only run so many head on your ranch, and when these things are ready to move you almost have to move 'em. You don't have the feed to hold 'em. That's where the ranchers have always been in a bind. You don't say, 'I want so much money for this steer I got here.' You say, 'How much will you give me for it?' You have to take the best offer you get, which isn't too good sometimes."

Taxes, mortgages, and price fluctuations aren't the only problems a modern day rancher has to face. As neighboring ranches are subdivided, people with urban and suburban backgrounds begin to dominate the countryside. And it's not just the people—it's their pets as well. "I've lost one hundred fifty head of sheep in the last four years by dogs," says Fred Wolf. "They just kill for the fun of it; they tear the throat out and get that one hot gush of blood and then go on to the next one."

Then there's coyotes. Coyotes kill the sheep, so they are poisoned; rabbits and rodents, formerly kept in check by the coyotes, eat the crops, so they too are poisoned. Sometimes it seems as if modern man's attempted answer to an unbalanced ecosystem is no ecosystem at all. Yet if you were a rancher who had just lost half your sheep, what would you do? The temptation for quick and easy solutions is certainly a strong one. Now the federal government wants to put controls on coyote killing, and the rancher quite understandably feels himself caught in a bind.

The particular problems faced by the ranchers and small landowners in northern California might not be identical to those faced by people of the Edges in other parts of the country. The terrain here is unique, as are some of the laws. But because our nation's land and resources are limited (or, to be more precise, because we now are beginning to understand the implications of our finitude), *all* small landowers are bound to be feeling the crunch in one way or another. The legal framework and taxation policies of each locality dictate certain ways in which country folk are most likely to make use of their land. If they appear to be raping the landscape, it might not be totally of their own free will; the people of the Edges, like people everywhere, are driven by laws and economic realities which appear to be handed down from above.

JOBS

Let's say that you are not a landowner, or that your land does not in itself provide you with a satisfactory income. To make a living you must find work. In every rural community there are a few service jobs that must be filled: postman, schoolteacher and school-bus driver, road contractor, storekeeper. But there has to be more—there has to be some basis for the economy. In my own backwoods area, the obvious choice for a local industry is logging. During the 1940's and 1950's, about twenty-five mills kept the area alive and hopping. Now only one remains. Many of the people who lived here during the logging boom have gone elsewhere in search of work. But the people who cared enough for the country to want to stay around still need work, and that naturally means they favor continued logging operations and oppose any attempts to stop them.

Or could you just live off the land, like they used to back in the old days? I doubt it. Most of the land in the backwoods is not good enough for intensive agriculture, or if it is it's in one of the few valleys where both land prices and taxes are exorbitant. The original homesteaders didn't have to contend with that. Nor did they require automotive transportation or many of the other expensive items that have become virtual necessities in to-day's world.

Perhaps the most successful homestead in my immediate area was the Etters' ranch, where five of the nine Etter brothers worked together with their families to raise their own food, mill their own lumber, and perform most of the other tasks necessary for a livelihood. The ranch even achieved some fame on account of Albert Etter's experimental work in developing new strains of apples and strawberries, several of which are still in use today. But the Etters' ranch is now virtually abandoned. The older generation (except for Albert's widow, Katherine) has all died off, while the younger generation never did take after their parents. I asked Katherine what happened.

"How come Ettersburg became unsettled? What happened to everyone?"

"Couldn't make a living off that land."

"But the older Etters did."

"That was different. A dollar was a dollar then. And they were settlers, and set in their ways. The young people wanted to get away. They came to school in here and then went out to work. A man can't work out and work on his place both. Comes home at night and too tired to work.

"They want things we did without. Those things weren't in existence then. People don't know how to do without things now. They want everything. Either that or it's 'Gimme, gimme, gimme.' "

In a few short sentences, Katherine had given a succinct statement of the Revolution of Rising Expectations. To satisfy the new needs, the younger generation of Etters took such jobs as delivering the mail and operating the local airport. And so it is throughout the countryside. Money and jobs are deemed absolute necessities.

But then again money always has been a valuable American commodity. From the beginning, the settlers hereabouts looked for ways to make their land turn a profit. Those in the forested but accessible valleys could harvest their timber, while those in the backcountry had to be content with a small surplus from the homesteads and a few hides and pelts from the woods. Then around the turn of the century, northwestern California experienced its first major industry: the bark was peeled off the tan oak for commercial use in tanning leather. Thousands of men spent their summers in bark-peeling camps scattered throughout the woods, transforming the previously untouched forest into money in their pockets. The unused trunks of the trees, meanwhile, were left to rot on the ground. "It looks just like my people lying around, lying around with all their skin cut off"— these were the words Nagaicho, the Indian Creator, supposedly used to describe the forests in the wake of the tanbark boom. It was the first serious conflict between ecology and economics here in the backcountry.

The tanbark industry began to fade around 1920 when synthetic tanning processes became widespread. But shortly thereafter, with the introduction of the ubiquitous and omnipotent Caterpillar, the previously inaccessible backwoods was opened to full-scale logging. The area boomed once again. Only twenty-five years later, however, virtually all the lumber had been taken and the logging boom was over. Left in the wake of the machine age's whirlwind tour through the backcountry were not only the death and debris in the forests, not only the salmon eggs buried beneath the eroded earth in the stream beds, but also the loggers themselves. Unemployment. Frank, an old-time logger, knows it well:

Machine age now. Working man is done for. Six Cats do more work than all the Chinamen in China. No manpower now. Don't need men no more. When a machine starts taking a man's place, what can a man do? People gone crazy with nothing to do. Damn it—I'm going crazy too.

All these young folks around, and no work. Then there's all these snags messing up the streams. Government should give them work cleaning up the country. Not twelve or thirteen hours like I used to do, just four or five hours.

Government's gotta change. We fought Hitler, now we got Hitler. Sitting in the White House smoking big cigars and making the poor people fight—and making money too.

Whether due to men or machines, the once virgin forests surrounding Frank's own modest home no longer exist. Never again will he have the opportunity to cut down trees which are twice as wide as he is tall.

Here, as elsewhere, economic interests seem to have wreaked ecological havoc. Yet there is something dangerously misleading about posing ecology and economics as inherently contradictory forces. Ecology, after all, deals with how various creatures make their living in an interdependent world; it is the economics of nature. If there is any contradiction, it is between *human* economic interests and *nonhuman* economic interests; for instance, people want to cut the trees, which is quite naturally against the best interests of the trees themselves. Indeed, modern man has come to shape the world so totally according to his own economic motives that the economics of other living species have been seriously jeopardized.

Even so, the differences between human and nonhuman interests are not always that great. In the final analysis, what were the economic consequences of the extensive logging of the backcountry? Poverty and unemployment. The natural resources have now been depleted, so it's harder than ever for people to make a living off the land. In desperation, individuals who are caught in the trap of their own economic system can perceive but one way out: to suck the land dry, to covet the last skimpy rewards that nature has to offer. Premature timber harvests, overgrazing, subdivision and development—these are the last dying attempts by the people of the backcountry to keep their heads abovewater.

The most basic contradiction, therefore, is not between economics and ecology, not even between man and nature, but rather between short-term and long-term perspectives. For twenty-five years, the timber harvest put money in the pockets of those who participated in it—but then what? It would take hundreds of years to regenerate the resources that were exhausted in that short period of time. Meanwhile, the folks in the backhills find themselves in an economic depression. The human ecology, as well as the natural ecology, has suffered—and no wonder, for is it not the same ecological system that links all living creatures in a given space on earth?

We can hardly blame the people of the backcountry for trying to make the most of what little they have left. City folk or country folk, conservationists or conservatives—people act according to what they perceive as their own best interests. Philosophical and moral concerns, though certainly important, are not always consistent with self-interest: a housewife, from the bastion of her electrically equipped suburban home, opposes a new power plant because it's a scar on the countryside; a lawyer, from the bastion of his paneled study, joins the fight to save the redwoods. An ecology organization, meanwhile, publishes a flashy magazine on unrecycled paper, because to do the same job on recycled paper would cost 10 percent more. Thus the people of the backcountry are not alone in letting personal convenience dictate their actions.

There is something sick going on in the name of economics: the virgin trees are cut; ranchers are driven off the land; coyotes are poisoned to protect sheep, while squirrels and rabbits, once coyote feed, are poisoned to protect crops. But who is to blame? Not, I suggest, the individual actors in a drama that has been written for them. The problem goes deeper, down to the roots of the economic system which gives the orders to chop the trees, develop the land, kill the animals.

People will be people. They play the game to win. The problem we face is how to change the rules of the game in such a way as to make the short-term interests of man more consistent with the long-term interests of man and nature alike.

Part Two

TREADING TIME IN TOWN

I might leave tomorrow. I got a four-wheel drive
and two cycles. But I'll probably come back. All
my friends are here. I've known them all my life.
All my family's here too. And I've already moved
up (I guess you'd call it that) to spotter.

—JIM, A MILLWORKER FOR
THE PACIFIC LUMBER COMPANY

3

Company Town

SCOTIA HAS ALWAYS BEEN a logging town. Everything in sight is naturally made of wood: the houses have identical planked siding; the yards are rimmed with picket fences; walkways made of well-weathered boards take the place of concrete sidewalks in the hillside districts. The houses don't all look exactly the same, but very nearly so. Each house, it appears, has been recently (but not *too* recently) painted in a nondescript shade of off-white. Outside, each yard is neatly trimmed; inside, the rooms have a standard decor which is simple, neat, and presentable. If suburban developments had sprung up forty or fifty years ago, this is what they might have been like. The garages and driveways are hidden in the back alleys—not as a matter of aesthetics but rather because the town was created at a time when it was not common for workers to own their own cars.

There is a strong hint of regimentation along the well-kept streets of Scotia, reminiscent of a military installation or an industrial town of years past. And no wonder, for Scotia is precisely that: one of the few remaining company towns in America, a self-contained creature of the Pacific Lumber Company. While most of the lesser mills have folded in recent years, the holdings of Pacific Lumber are so vast that it will always have second-growth forests to harvest even after the last of the virgin timber is gone. Indeed, Scotia is the home of the largest redwood mill in California, and thus in the world. Incredibly massive machinery has been developed specifically to cope with the seventy-ton logs: saws as big as trees, conveyor belts that

43

never stop, giant claws that lift the largest conceivable logs with the greatest of ease. Whole buildings shake as the logs collide. The intense noise and vibration of the entire operation leaves each worker virtually isolated on his job, unable to communicate with his neighbor. The workers' only reality is the speed, power, and tyranny of the machines—and of the wood.

Everything in town is owned by the company: streets, shops, houses, church, and school. They rent or lease much of it, but control is ultimately in their hands. They determine who is allowed to move in, and into which houses they will move. If the lawns are not kept up to par, the company gardener will be sent in to do the job. If the company doesn't want noisy parties at night, if it would prefer not to have old cars being worked on in the streets, all it has to do is say so. If it wants the houses painted a certain way, that's the way it will be done. And, most basically, it has the power to say "No"—to fire the head of the household, which, since only employees of the Pacific Lumber Company are allowed to reside in town, is equivalent to a notice of eviction.

There is not room enough in town for all of the company's one thousand workers plus their families; a long waiting list has thus been formed of those who are ready and willing to move in. Some selection has to be made, but not necessarily on a first come, first serve basis. Instead, the privilege of living in Scotia is a reward to the faithful, to the ardent worker, or to the man with family connections or "pull."

Why does everyone want to live in Scotia? Because it's cheap. Rents for a complete house are as low as $55 a month, and rarely above $85. Water, sewerage, and garbage collection are all free. "If I could rent a place over there," says a young worker, "it'd be great. There's not much action, but for surviving . . ." With rents so cheap, what does the company get out of it? "They get all their money back," says the worker. "And they get to keep control."

Inexpensive housing is not the only benefit Pacific Lumber offers its employees. Each year, the workers get a bonus which increases in accord with how long they have worked for P.L.: 3 percent of the yearly wage the first time around, increasing up to 7 percent for the fifth year and thereafter. There are seven paid holidays and four-week vacations with pay for five-year men. There is a pension plan, in which the company will double the employee's contribution, and an investment plan, in which stock in P.L. can be purchased at reduced rates. The whole family gets 80 percent medical coverage. A thousand-dollar scholarship is offered to college students coming from company families. Each Christmas, the kids are given a free toy and a jar of candy; when they reach eighteen, they are given five dollars and cut off the rolls, for they are by then ready to become workers themselves.

"The best all-around benefits for any mill in the county," says another young worker. The pay itself is also competitive: $3.92 an hour is the lowest on the line; $5.13 an hour is common among second-year men. That's about the same as in the handful of other mills which have managed to remain in business. "The companies," says a retired foreman, "they all sleep together."

Pacific Lumber has a vested interest in looking after its own: to maintain a stable work force. Its turnover is less than 6 percent per year, which is quite remarkable among millworkers, who, as a group, tend to be more transient. The general policy is to keep it all within the family—to hire relatives and friends of proven, faithful employees. "It's not how much you know, but who you know," says a newcomer to the payroll. "One thing you can say about the way things work over there," adds his friend, "is if you have a lot of pull . . . Yep, that's the way they work—with pull." But these young workers are not complaining, for that is how they got their jobs. I have yet to talk with a worker who got on through the waiting list; they all seem to have fathers or uncles or someone who pulled the strings. This, then, is another benefit the company has to offer: guaranteed employment for the upcoming generation.

It is only in relation to the company, however, that individuals are seen as beneficial. Once retired (or, for that matter, injured), a worker and his family are no longer allowed to reside in Scotia. At sixty-five, a man can expect to lose not only his job but his home. There are thus no real old-timers in Scotia; it is perhaps the largest community around that lacks a graveyard.

. . .

What, besides work, is there to do in a company town? There is a swimming pool and a gymnasium, open to all employees and their families. There are organized sports, with the men divided into teams according to their stations at work: B re-mill, A green chain, B green chain, machine shop, factory, B kilns, plywood, never sweats (foremen and management). The ball games are taken almost as seriously as work itself. "They damn near kill themselves," says a housewife. "But I guess they have fun." When I ask a young worker in the plywood mill if he would prefer the night shift, he responds, "No way. I've got too much happening." What, I ask him, does he have happening? "Oh, Pop Warner, Little League. Stuff like that."

For the older workers or the less physically inclined, there is the company Men's Club. For seventy-five cents a month, members can enjoy pool, table tennis, and cards, or take advantage of the spacious reading room rimmed with hard-backed chairs and stocked with a wide assortment of periodical literature.

What about the women? "They have reducing clubs with swimming and weight lifting and things like that," says Mary, a former housewife who has since been divorced and left town. "Then they have their coffee klatches and Avon parties and Tupperware parties. They all go to the same parties with the same people and build up points. A few of them work, or maybe have a child-care center or go shopping together." The women's role is clearly defined, and it does not include work in the mill. But at least here in Scotia, a small town par excellence, they are not left isolated within the confines of their private homes as they might be in the cities or suburbs. "I guess they do the same as they do anywhere else, but they do it together."

Opportunities for the kids seem limited. The movie theater has long since closed down, while the skating rink was washed out by a flood and never replaced. The attractions of the modern world of youth are nowhere to be found in this self-contained society. Even the nearby woods are made inaccessible by the Eel River on one side and the freeway on the other. "For me, it's dull," explains Mary, who was raised as a company kid.

"Every building is the same. The only word I can use to describe it is 'sterile.' And everybody knows everybody else. They all work together and they all go to the same parties and do everything together. Just one big clan. It's just like a colony." But not all the kids feel this way. Many, perhaps even most, will get married right after high school and settle down to the life-long business of working in the mill or raising children in a millworking town.

Men, women, or children—nobody can be totally satisfied with the limited diversions of a company town. Just across the Eel River bridge, however, and less than a mile from the mills, lies Scotia's alter ego: Rio Dell. This is where the rest of the workers live—those not fortunate enough to find housing in Scotia, or those desiring more freedom. Rio Dell is everything that Scotia is not. There are a disproportionate number of clubs and liquor stores and beauty salons, where people can drink, dance, or indulge themselves in a little bit of pomp. With Highway 101 bisecting the center of town, the automobile economy is dominant. The cafes are all closed down, while the drive-ins (which are conspicuously absent in neighboring Scotia) do a booming business.

Back in the old days, when Rio Dell was mostly farm land, its name was Wildwood. That was when over two thousand workers, almost all of them single, were crammed into bunk-houses and tents and fed in cookhouses over in Scotia. Gambling houses and bars and cathouses naturally sprang up in Wildwood to service the needs and desires of the workers. As the loggers and millworkers gradually became more family-oriented, the less acceptable of these amusements disappeared—but the bars remained.

Rio Dell spills forth with the unstructured life that Scotia denies. It is a totally unplanned hodgepodge of small, old, wooden bungalows, modern ticky-tacky shacks, and standard mid-century ranch houses. The roads can't quite decide whether they're paved or not. Lawns are often untrimmed and on occasion nonexistent. Doorways, many of them facing right onto the streets, are commonly left open as the smells of dinner and the sounds of kids permeate the air. Old cars in various states of disrepair are constantly being tinkered with outside the homes.

Back in Scotia, meanwhile, the doors are closed and the kids and cars tucked neatly away where they belong. Partly, this is because the company simply won't allow untidiness of any sort; partly it is the nature of the people whom the company has selected as its tenants. But it is also due to the effect an environment can have on human behavior: if you live in Scotia, it just doesn't seem *right* to leave your door ajar, your grass unclipped, or your old clunker parked out front.

How do the workers themselves feel about the company that dominates their lives? Jim, age twenty-two, went to work in the mill right out of high school. Since he comes from a good Pacific Lumber family, there was no problem in getting a job. "I don't like working any more than anyone else," he says over a beer after work. "But if you have to work, you might as well do it right."

"You must get pretty good at it after a while," I suggest.

"It's not so much getting good at it as getting used to it. You work eight hours a day, five days a week, so you have to. Then if you don't keep up the pace, they either fire you or try to put you somewhere else. They call that the 'rat race.' When you first start out, they move you around. They stick you in wherever they need you. Then they find you a permanent place. They don't move you around much after that at P.L. There are jobs that are interesting, but it takes time to work your way up to one. You know, it's hard to get your mind into mill work. It takes someone who doesn't really give a shit. Hey," he calls over to a friend with a flip-top can in his hand, "you got anything good to say about P.L.?"

"There's not much to say about it," comes the reply, "except that you can't say anything bad or you're out of a job. I want to get a place in Scotia, so I'm not talking." Assured that his name won't be used, the second young man changes his mind and agrees to speak his piece. "I want to move around. I started there on spraying, now I drive forklift, but that's all I've ever done. What I'd like to do is move around to five or six different mills and work on different jobs and see how it's all done. That's one thing I can say—they don't move you around.

"I think almost everyone who works there would like to buck P.L., but there's nothing you can do about it. I think things would be a lot different if there was a union. The way I see it, when you work for the union you work for yourself, not for someone else. No, I don't think anyone really likes the company. But they have things pretty well all sewed up."

"But you can't complain," adds a third beer-drinking worker. "You work less than thirty hours and you get paid for forty. That's with breakdowns and everything," he explains.

"Do you hope for breakdowns?" I ask.

"Sure, I always do. But I'll tell you another thing. You take a guy who's been there five years and they pretty well look after him. They'll get him a house pretty quick."

"Yeah, I guess so," concludes the union-leaning forklift driver. "I don't exactly like P.L., but I still can't think of anything better either."

Some of the older men are more generous with their praise. Albert Kewitt, known by everyone simply as "Dutch," started in at P.L. sweeping floors in 1923. He had come from Germany via China and Japan and could speak no English. Slowly he learned the language, came to understand the machinery, and worked his way up to foreman and eventually to head millwright. If a machine broke down anywhere in the mill, it was his job to fix it. Even after he had retired, they'd call him down for advice. Now, as ever, Dutch's life centers on the company. "I still go down there three or four times a week. I go have coffee and doughnuts for breakfast, go see what's going on and talk to the boys."

Dutch's friend Herb also worked his way up from a floor sweeper in 1928 to a gang sawyer upon retirement. "If you want to work," says Herb, "there ain't a better place around, I'll tell you that. That's the best company in the county. They beat them union mills all to pieces. You get more than union pay, and you get all the benefits and bonuses and everything. If they fire you, there's something wrong with you. No, that's the best company anywhere—*if* you want to work."

Herb and Dutch can remember when conditions weren't so good. "Used to be two holidays a year," says Herb. "Christmas and Thanksgiving. Christmas you had the whole day off, and they gave you an extra hour off Thanksgiving to eat."

"I worked on Christmas Eve," adds Dutch. "Christmas Day we had off, so Christmas Eve I had to work and we worked to five o'clock in the morning, pouring cement for the log dump there. The manager, he comes down around about midnight with some coffee and doughnuts and some pie and we had that to eat and then back to work again."

It wasn't until World War II, with the labor shortage and the increasing power of the unions, that Pacific Lumber started its more liberalized program of benefits. In 1945 the mill was shut down for several months by a strike, but the company finally won. Its strategy since then has been simple: offer the workers just a little more than the unions and union shops can afford to match. P.L. is just big enough—and rich enough—to pull it off.

The differing attitudes toward the company closely approximate the different stations of the workers: the foremen seem to like it, while others are not so sure. As in any large-scale industrial operation, there are subtle gradations of status: those who wear hard hats and those who do not, those who are free to move around and those who are not, those who work at skilled jobs and those who do not, those who do physical labor and those who do not. ("When you walk through and see somebody doing nothing, you know he's getting good money," says a second-year man.) And in Scotia, as in any small town, there are subtle gradations of status based upon where one lives—up in the hills or down near the tracks. P.L. is able to manipulate all of this to its best advantage, offering rewards not only of higher jobs but also of better housing to those who toe the line, and thus encouraging an obedient work force. "How long," I ask a worker, "does it take to become a foreman?" "It depends . . . if you know somebody. Or maybe you'll work all your life and never move up at all." The company, in a word, is the boss.

. . .

Throughout California and across the nation, many if not most of the small towns are creatures of the automobile culture. For teen-agers everywhere, the private car has meant instant liberation through unlimited mobility. And the small-town landscapes pay tribute to their liberator: neonized auto rows extend outward in every direction, creeping slowly into the once placid countryside. On weekend nights hordes of youngsters flock to these sprawling circuses of drive-ins and gas stations for their recreation; they cruise, they drag, or, most basically, they simply remain on the move. Motion, speed, change—this is the mood of the mid-twentieth century, and the small-town folks do not wish to be left behind.

It has been scarcely fifty years, however, since cars began to dominate the countryside—and the texture of social life as well. Without automotive transportation, there was no way a person in the early 1900's could traverse large distances on his way to and from the job every day. People, of necessity, lived near their place of work, so working communities and living communities were not far apart. With the widespread availability of the automobile, however, came the equally widespread practice of commuting. Today, the people who work in a given factory, office, or institution of any sort commonly live ten, twenty, or even fifty miles away from one another. Conversely, the residents of any particular neighborhood do not necessarily inhabit the same workaday world. Even in most small towns, people have adapted to a commuting way of life. The opportunities for forming a tight-knit community are thus severely limited by this schizophrenic existence.

Not so in Scotia. Here it is almost as if the automobile had never been invented. There are no drive-ins to be found in town, nor does creeping urban sprawl stretch outward into the woods. Driveways and garages, instead of dominating the front lawns, are relegated to the back alleys. The men walk to work, where they can expect to see all their neighbors. The women, meanwhile, have more than physical proximity to bind them together: they are all millworkers' wives. And all the kids are reared with a single common vision of what it means to be an adult: to work in the mill, or to raise a millworking family.

It is therefore not surprising that many of the young men eventually get jobs with P.L., or that many of the young women eventually marry the young millworking men. The upcoming generation, for the most part, seems willing to pick up the torch, to carry on the line. Kinship ties are strong. Sons and daughters speak respectfully of their parents, and youngsters generally choose to live close to the homes they know so well.

People here have roots, such as they are. Jim, for instance, could probably make a go at it anywhere, but he chooses to stay at P.L. "It's livable," he says. "You don't have to put up with all the crap down in the cities. I wouldn't live there if you paid me. When I see the way people are down there—they get into traffic jams or something. . . . Well, I love to go down there and fool around, but the people are so uptight. It'd rack my nerves."

"Then you're pretty well settled up here?"

"Who knows? I might leave tomorrow. I got a four-wheel drive and two cycles. But I'll probably come back. All my friends are here. I've known them all my life. All my family's here too. And I've already moved up (I guess you'd call it that) to spotter."

Such an attitude has become a rarity in today's fast-changing world. How strange that strong ties to one's family and childhood friends, once the backbone of American social life, can now be seen only in a few isolated settings out here on the Edges, far removed from metropolitan circles. A young man from the suburbs is not really expected to get a house down the block from his folks. Instead, he is likely to move where his company or his profession sends him. And even in most small towns, many if not most of the youth can be expected to migrate to the cities in search of work and opportunity. But here in Scotia, there are always plenty of jobs available to the members of a good company clan. Paternalistic P.L., in its own way, has shielded the town folk from the economic pressures affecting the rest of the countryside. By offering jobs to the members of the younger generation it provides a setting in which whole families can remain intact.

There is something faintly historical about Scotia. It is not the self-conscious type of history found in restored tourist towns, nor is it the ancient history of centuries past. Perhaps it dates back to a time before the automobile, when working and living communities were contiguous; perhaps to a time before TV, when a small town's life was its own; perhaps to a time before crime-in-the-streets, for there is no crime in Scotia even now; perhaps to a time before black power and women's liberation, for the workers at the mill are virtually all white and male; perhaps to a time before ranch-house suburbia, when plain-planked siding was as modern as one cared to get; perhaps to a time before color film, when the world was all in black, gray, and white (for that is how Scotia still looks today). Scotia stands as a rock amid the fluidity of our modern world. The almighty company provides a shelter under which the cosmopolitan tendencies of the Metropolis can be successfully resisted and small-town life can continue in perpetuity.

History moves slowly here. The portrait overlooking the entranceway to the Men's Club is of General Eisenhower, in triumphant salute, returning from the war. That feels just about right—1945—although we might just call it "sometime not too long ago." The clock is held in check, if only for thirty years, and only in some respects. Nothing less powerful than mighty P.L. could tamper thus with time.

4

A Victorian Village
in Old Cream City

FERNDALE HAS ALWAYS BEEN a dairy and ranching town. The Cape Mendocino hill country to the south is populated only by large herds of sheep and cattle and by a few isolated, well-established ranchers; the Eel River delta to the north and east is perhaps the richest dairyland in California. The lush green pastures of the valley floor are interrupted sporadically by gnarled cypress trees reaching with contorted movements into the fog, by charred stumps dating back to a time when the land was first cleared, or by towering hedges which have been stripped of their leaves by the winds they were supposed to stop. The dairy herds appear abnormally healthy on these frost-free fields which are blessed by the moist, temperate air from the nearby Pacific. The old, well-peopled farmhouses are intricately conceived, with numerous porches, sheds, and towers; the lines of the old, well-used barns are simple but gracefully efficient. The houses are decently maintained but have not been recently painted; the gray weathered wood on the barns has never been painted at all.

Surrounding Ferndale is a rural community which still belongs to itself. Agriculture has been modernized, but it has not yet been totally taken over by the bank. The one-room schoolhouse is still a living reality. Exceptional dairy cows such as Silken Lady's Ruby of F. (who gave 10,936 pounds of fat and

196,457 pounds of milk in her twenty-one years on earth) are buried with all the glory of martyred heroines. The Future Farmers of America, perhaps the most active organization around, has erected its own special sign welcoming visitors to town.

Ferndale itself has more the appearance of a nineteenth-century European village than a twentieth-century American town. It is nestled cozily into the valley at the foot of forested hills. Its most prominent points are neither office buildings nor neon signs, but towering church spires reaching for God in the sky. There is no auto row and little suburban development to separate the town from the countryside: the houses end abruptly at the hills or lead directly into the pastures. Cornfields and potato patches frequently replace front yards, while cows can peer into the windows of those who live at the end of the block. There is a wooden sidewalk on the north end of Main Street which follows along a gently flowing stream. On the south end of town is a terraced cemetery large enough to hold the remains of every person who ever lived in Ferndale—and it probably does, for this is a tight-knit community.

"It's all old families," says Amelia Alward, a retired school-teacher in her eighties, who has been in the area since 1893. "All of them. It's very cliquish. It's hard to break in. And they won't let in a Safeway or anything like that. Of course, they do allow us to put our names in their telephone book. We have two types of names: first there was the Hansons and Petersons and so on; then the Portuguese came in and leased the dairies and now we have the Mendes and Mirandas and like that." It has been generations since the last wave of European immigrants arrived, but ethnic identities are still maintained. There is both a Portuguese and a Danish Hall, each with its own brotherhoods and sisterhoods. On the Day of Ascension the Portuguese hold their Holy Ghost celebration, which includes a colorful parade through town; in midsummer the Scandinavians hold their own festival at the fairgrounds, complete with folk dancing and feasting. "They still call themselves Danes and so on," says another elderly native, "but where it used to be sort of a sensitive matter, now it's not so at all."

Ferndale's most visible departure from twentieth-century Americana, and its most concrete link with the past, is its Victorian architecture. The town is full of false fronts and fake columns, bay windows and elaborately carved woodwork inscribed with meaningless insignia and painted bright colors (yellow, purple, red, green, orange, pink) to accentuate the patterns. The houses appear ostentatious because of their decorative, nonfunctional designs, and yet, simply because they are old, they also appear rather quaint.

Each house has its own history and individual character. The Gum Drop House, named after five cypress trees in front which have been clipped and sculptured like poodles into the shape of five huge pieces of candy, was built by pioneer A. Berding in 1875 and is inhabited today by his granddaughter, Gertrude Clausen. Unlike most other Ferndale structures, it is still painted white and retains much of its original furnishings. Just around the corner is the Gingerbread Mansion, Ferndale's pride and joy, which was built by a prosperous doctor at the turn of the century and since then used as a hospital, an American Legion post, and once again as a private dwelling. It reeks delightfully of Old World pomp: porches, walkways, balconies, verandas, solariums, turrets, and outside stairways; delicate gingerbread designs painted in muted yellow and salmon; heavy wooden doors painted yellow and black; imitation lace curtains at the windows; a wicker chair on the porch shaped like an hourglass underneath and a fan on top; two cement hounds flanking the entranceway, each with a fruit basket hanging from its jaws; a fastidiously manicured English garden with brick walkways, trimmed lawns, hundreds of varieties of flowers, miniature hedges clipped in perfect geometric shapes, a four-tier goldfish fountain topped by a cherub hugging a fish and rimmed by a cast-iron chain to keep out the elves; and, last but not least, a touch of local California flavor—a giant palm tree. A total environment has been created, with only a single aluminum-framed screen door on the service entrance to betray its mid-twentieth century reality.

The shops on Main Street have a similar flourish, for the

Victorian mood has taken over the town. On each old building hangs a plaque telling of its origin and prior use. But where drugstores and hardware stores used to stand, now there are mostly art galleries and gift shops, for Ferndale has become something of an artists' colony in the past ten years. There are no fewer than fifteen stores on Main Street that feature paintings, wire sculptures, pottery, house plants, leatherwork, candles, yarns, and jewelry—and a single grocery store. Every spring there is a week-long art festival with music in the streets and a "kinetic sculpture race" between giant replicas of inch worms and turtles and stupendous bicycle contraptions of all sorts. Unlike art fairs elsewhere, however, the festival here is a true community event: old-timers participate by organizing the activities and by displaying their own household skills—quilting, crocheting, knitting, tatting, spinning, weaving, embroidering, and stuffing toys. Indeed, the festival itself was the creation of some of Ferndale's influential natives who also happened to be artists.

What was Ferndale like before the recent immigration of artists from the outside world? "They had about two of everything: two hardware stores, two lawyers, and so on," explains sixty-seven-year-old Viola McBride, an artist and a rancher whose grandfather was one of Ferndale's first settlers. "It was pretty well filled. They had more of regular things. But then we had two floods, in '55 and '64. While they didn't reach the town, they really clobbered the countryside, which affects the town. Oh, it was just practically deserted. You could rent a building for ten or twenty dollars a month, where now you'd pay over a hundred." With cheap rents, a mild climate, the beautiful countryside, and Victorian flavor, the artists naturally gravitated to the area.

Even Ferndale's Victorian flavor, strangely enough, is of fairly recent origin. The people of Ferndale used to be just as eager as anyone else to streamline their town, but then a handful of natives such as Viola McBride, well endowed with significant real estate holdings, became actively involved in the restoration of old houses.

You used to get those gingerbread buildings for just a song. There was one painter who used to say, "It won't cost you any more to have a nice modern front than it would to buy the paint for all this junk." So they'd just sheer the front off and they'd stucco it. There's several buildings there you can see that are just flat like that.

During the war, the Ivanhoe burned. The fire gutted the back part of it, but the front was still all right. All these people just couldn't wait to get this gingerbread off this old eyesore. Well, I thought, it's old, it's original. They're good buildings because the fire laws back in the nineties said you had to nail one two-by-six or two-by-something right onto the other. So you have a solid wooden wall on the outsides of all these buildings. They may be parallelograms, but they're still pretty solid.

So Hazel Waldner and I (she ran the *Enterprise* while her husband was in the war) knew very well what would happen to the Ivanhoe. In fact, they had already condemned it the day after the fire. But Hazel and I used to go to the Chamber of Commerce and fight. We went to the hardheaded old Swiss and we said, "Isn't that marvelous! The front didn't burn. The front is just like in the old country." We said that it was a landmark, and wasn't he lucky to have a landmark in his backyard. By the time we finished, nobody was going to cut it off. So he studded up the back of it so it was no longer condemned, and it's still there.

The thing is, people are inclined to say something is hopeless; actually, if the walls aren't rotten it isn't hopeless. It's easy enough to put in a foundation and a roof. Of course, they're always crooked. I did have one carpenter who was so fussy about everything being square he just nearly went crazy. Out where we live we had to take an inch or more off one end of the door and put it on the bottom.

But the biggest problem I ever had was saving the old rectory. They were changing priests, because one of them got too old. The interim priest was a fat little guy who didn't like Ferndale *at all*, and he certainly didn't like this rectory. It was cold, but it would have been perfectly easy to put central heating in it. Anyway, he evidently had the ear of the bishop, who was quite a builder—I guess he about broke the diocese. So he said the rectory had to come down.

I've never seen Ferndale more united. Usually they're fighting about everything. But they wrote letters to the bishop, to the Pope. Catholics and non-Catholics both, although the Catholics were a little more outraged than the Protestants since they had to pay the bill.

Then I got to thinking: well, the thing is to get it on the newsstand some way. A friend had looked into having postcards made of what she painted. Now, I paint, so I painted a picture of the whole thing. I'd park out front with this awful-looking old rig I had then and painted it. People would stop in the middle of the street and discuss with loud voices: "Isn't that awful!" "The poor rectory!" And cursing the bishop. The Catholics, as I say, were worse than the Protestants.

Another thing that happened was a bunch of Catholics got together and wrote a letter to the Pope and signed it. But they didn't want to put their return address on it, so I had to put my address on it.

So I guess they finally decided I was making more trouble than anybody else, so the priest called up and said, if they gave it to me, would I move it? Well, just standing there flat-footed on the phone, I said, "Oh, yes."

It cost a lot to move it. I had all kinds of troubles. It had to go to somewhere on that side of Main Street because it wouldn't fit under the wires. But I finally got it moved to a lot right across from the graveyard, and that's where it is now.

Now, nearly everybody in Ferndale is in favor of historical preservation. A strict zoning ordinance has been passed which requires all new building or renovations of old buildings to be done in a manner consistent with the Victorian motif of the town. Claiming credit for the zoning laws is three-time mayor Jack Tipple, a small, mild-mannered automobile dealer who plays drums on Saturday nights and dabbles in cinematography whenever he can get the time. "I called in a professional city planner from San Jose," he says, "at my own expense to see what could be done." That was in 1966, when the tide in Ferndale had already turned toward preservation. Today, Jack Tipple is proud of the attention his town has received because of its historical flavor. "*Sunset* magazine and Walter Cronkite have done features on us," he boasts. "We get to feeling like we're being looked at in a zoo. But we sort of get a kick out of it here on our corner. Once we kept a record of it: 187 people came off the street on a Saturday afternoon to use our rest rooms."

A few years back, the people of Ferndale all got together for a gigantic paint-in on their historical treasures. A color consultant was hired and a tentative plan was prepared; a town meeting was held at the fairgrounds at which the mural of Ferndale-to-be was unveiled. Then one weekend Main Street was closed off and the whole town painted itself, the gas station included. The colors were slightly more muted than those that have been added since, yet they were still more lively than the historically authentic off-white and tan-brown combinations which were predominant back in the old days. Ferndale wanted a touch of the past, but it did not wish to be considered too dull.

Agriculture, art, and historical architecture—it's a peculiar combination indeed. The new face of the town has been accepted by everyone, but the new alliance among the people themselves is sometimes uneasy: the old ranchers and dairymen, for instance, don't fully appreciate the take-over of Main Street by the newcomers. "It's a lot of people coming north from L.A., San Francisco—most of 'em with some money," explains a native of the town. "They can afford to kick back a little and play games."

"You can't eat a painting," remarks a crusty old rancher on his way to deposit a side of home-butchered beef in his locker at the Ferndale Meat Company.

"Christ, it's just a small town," complains another old salt outside the feed store, his floppy hat pulled down over his unshaven face, his jeans pulled down below his paunch, and his work shirt rolled up to reveal forearms the size of biceps. "Just hippies here now. Nothing to come to town for. My wife don't care to drink anyways. I've only been in twice this year. I wanna get something, I just go on up to Eureka."

Yet with time the newcomers are slowly becoming more accepted by many of the natives. Jack Mays, another native artist, explains the changes he's seen in the few years since the artists moved in:

In the beginning, most people took it pretty rough. Of course, a lot of the *real* old ranchers couldn't give a damn less, one way or the other, 'cause they don't come into town that often. And the way the art managed to take over Main Street was all the other businesses went defunct. So obviously they weren't supporting Main Street anyway; what happened there was of no consequence to them. But the people who took it the toughest were the other merchants on Main Street. And they had a point. They had a nice little situation, and it was being changed. It didn't matter what the change was—there were just so many new faces coming in. And at that time there was the big hippie concerns. I don't think it was the art thing they objected to so much as it was the almost catastrophic changes they felt they were going through. And the big hippie thing. Because Ferndale was already into the art festival and such before all the new artists got here.

Now, the people that did move in are such an integral part of the community that it's hard to remember who's a native and who's not. It's just like a wave of immigration, and now they've all settled in. But they all came at one time, which was a little bit of a trauma.

Right now at the Chamber of Commerce there's a new blend, they got a new kind of promotional thing to get everybody reinvolved and thinking together as a business community. The president's a new gal here that runs the yarn shop, and the vice-president's the old jeweler. And they get more people down to those meetings now than they ever had.

Almost every artist here now, the reason they're still here is the fact that they've gotten local support in terms of buying their products. For example, one of the old hard guys just went down and bought a squash-blossom necklace for his wife. Pretty expensive, too. I don't sell anything to tourists; all my sales are to people in the county, and more and more to people in Ferndale. Of all the people I know and deal with socially, very few of them are artists. They're dairymen, or bulldozer operators, or . . . In fact, that's one of the reasons I do the kind of sculpture I do, where I deal with people and their occupations. A guy'll come out and he'll bulldoze our roads and do some clearing for us, and I'll get all excited and I'll do a sculpture of him. And then *he's* all excited, because all of a sudden there's an art about him. It brings art down to something he understands and knows.

The arts here are reaching a practical level, based on the needs of Ferndale and the county. For example, the guy that started a kind of artsy-craftsy leather shop now is swinging over to making saddles. So we've got a saddlemaker in town, and there's a definite need for guys that make harnesses and saddles and things like that. And the guy that opened up the little artsy-craftsy plant shop swung into a florist shop, which is as basic a business as there is. Send flowers to funerals and stuff like that. So a lot of these places are swinging into a kind of "new realism" for Ferndale.

In my generation—I got out of school in '56—everybody in my generation left. They went to the cities and things like that. That's just about the time the Ferndale business area died, because people were going off to bigger and better things. But now the kids are starting to stay around. They're not awed by the big world. You get more sons going into carpentry because their old man's doing that. People aren't leaving the way they were, and a lot of people like myself came back.

The artists, in their own way, have given a boost to the economy: they have made the business of historical restoration appear financially profitable as outsiders of aesthetic sensibilities, seeking a glimpse of Victorian treasures, flock into town and visit their shops. Forward-looking citizens of Ferndale can now look into the past and find there the resources to make their town prosper. Bypassed by both the railroad and the highway, Ferndale had the good fortune to be bypassed also by the building boom of the postwar years when America was being refashioned after its own image. Because it was forgotten then, it stands to be remembered today.

But there are dangers inherent in an economy geared to tourism. What would happen to the farmers and everyone else if, as has been periodically rumored, Rockefeller interests were to buy up the town and make it into a national spectacle? The old buildings might remain, but what would it mean to the basically agrarian way of life? Would fancy antique stores line the roads where ranches now stand? History, indeed, is a touchy affair. Is it the buildings? The artifacts? The people? The culture? What good would it do to save the houses yet drive their inhabitants away?

Fortunately, it will probably never happen that way. For behind Main Street's antique-mod veneer of newly painted Victorian architecture and art shops, the "real" Ferndale, the farming town, continues as always. The feedstore, the meat company, the hardware store, the lumberyard—the business of ranching is still dominant, even if it is not as evident. Some of the old shops might have closed, but the really important ones, from the ranchers' point of view, did not. "The art is really sort of a surface thing," says Jack Mays. "It takes up more room in terms of shops, but they only account for a small percentage of the volume of transactions here in town. The hardware store will probably turn over as much business in one day as all the art stores will do in a month."

Whatever happens in town, the farmers seem to hang on. Even the damage from the floods did not induce them to sell out. "It's a whole different breed of people here," says a worker in the feedstore, a native who knows the place well. "They're tight, very tight. People pretty much stick to themselves. They got their own little cliques, groups of other farmers like themselves. Won't none of 'em sell, even in hard times. Most cases, it's been in the family for generations. They try to keep it on just for sentimental value. There's these corporations, conglomerates, come up from down below trying to buy out a ranch—well, the neighbors just get together and put in a higher bid. Tie up the land that way. Why, I want to get a ranch myself someday, but even if I had the money there ain't none around that's for sale." And so it goes. In other parts of the California countryside, ranches are being offered for sale at an alarming rate as the pressures on the land increase. But not here. Perhaps the most significant aspect of Ferndale's business community, although certainly not the most obvious, is its paucity of real estate brokers.

5

Summer Festivals:
Rodeo, Fair, and Wildwood Days

MAIN STREET IS LINED with people. They swarm over the parked cars and perch on the tops of the roofs. This is Fortuna's biggest day of the year: the Rodeo Parade is coming.

The excitement has been building all week. The soap-box derby, square dance, and pie-eating contest—these were but preliminaries leading up to the grand climax of the rodeo itself. The front page of the paper could speak of nothing else. Local merchants, assessing the mood of the season, have been advertising accordingly: "We've lassoed a whole store full of fashion values for Fortuna Rodeo Days"; "Don't get roped into not carrying adequate insurance"; "Up in this country, we use the B of A brand"; "Head your savings to Johnson's Corral."

So here they are: the entire population of Fortuna, and more. They wear well-chosen sports clothes and western hats that look like they have been brought out of storage just for the occasion. The morning fog is beginning to lift, and the parade commences with an earsplitting wail of police sirens. The flag-carrying senior members of the VFW and American Legion are followed closely by Fortuna's pride and joy: the eighty-man Volunteer Fire Department with their eight shiny new fire trucks and a horse-driven antique just for show. After that there's a band on a truck, and then a float which features the Dairy Princess riding a rocking horse. The Grange comes by in a hay wagon, with the men holding pitchforks and the women wearing bonnets and granny dresses. Everyone tosses out penny candies to the kids.

One after another they come—individuals and families who are proud to display the fruits of their historical hobbies. Being in the parade is fun. Anyone can enter. Mr. and Mrs. Hyde, for instance, are in the parade every year. This time it is a stage-coach decorated with no fewer than 5,500 pink, white, and yellow Kleenex flowers. The flowers took a long time to make, but the Hydes had their six children and fourteen grandchildren to help them out. After expending all that energy, they usually manage to win a trophy or ribbon of some sort. "But we don't do it for that," claims Mrs. Hyde. "We do it for the grandkids. They have so much fun."

Most entries, however, have ulterior motives. A tepee and a dozen kids dressed in elaborate Indian costumes go by under a banner that reads, "Tired of Living in a Tepee?" Yes, it's an ad for a realty company. Twenty more kids walk down the street carrying transistors; their sign advertises a local radio station. There are more ads for a used-car lot, a retirement home, a building supply company. And of course there are politicians as well, waving to the crowd like everyone else.

Scattered throughout the parade are drivers of dragsters and dune buggies, revving their motors and spitting out exhaust into the faces of the onlookers. Imitating their older mentors are a score of young drivers of Yamahas and Hondas, all members of the "Mighty Mini Racing Association of Northern California." The oldest of the kids is about fourteen, the youngest is only six. Each is seated on an appropriately sized motorcycle, and they all wear helmets and jackets with their club's name inscribed on the back.

Then come the horses—some two hundred of them. Everyone who owns a horse rides in the parade: some are members of clubs, some are not; some are in costume, some are not. After the horses come the logging trucks, hauling huge specimens of virgin timber through the center of town. The trucks squash the excrement from the horses that preceded them, giving Main Street the aroma of a barnyard. Behind two tandem trucks carrying full loads of lumber, three little girls dressed in old-time bonnets are dragging a small handcart with frying pans and a wooden model of a gun. "Redwood Bootery Has the Western Look," reads their sign. The girls are coughing and choking from the fumes of the trucks, and one of them has her hands over her ears to lessen the noise. They are the only sad faces around.

The parade is headed for the rodeo grounds, where the awards will be granted and the rodeo itself will commence. The crowd follows along, drifting away from Main Street and into the grandstands. There are a thousand, perhaps two thousand, spectators. Not everyone, however, has to pay to see the rodeo. Kids stand on the tops of the fences where the animals are kept, while young men with cowboy hats sit on the cabs of their pickups, drinking beer and sniffing snuff. Nearer to the action than the folks in the stands, they can hear the sounds of hooves and breathe the dust of the arena. They are behind stage, as it were, part and parcel of the rodeo that they hope someday to join.

The grandstand, like grandstands everywhere, is filled with vendors and the stench of beer. But there is something different here. The atmosphere is more personal, more intimate. People call out to their friends; everybody seems to know everybody else. The competing cowboys mix with the crowd, wearing their spurs and sometimes their numbers on their backs. There are men and women in almost equal proportions, and an abundance of children. The Fortuna Rodeo is clearly a family affair. The concessions are run by local social organizations: the VFW sells the beer, while the women's clubs peddle their homemade cookies. It is a home-town crowd, indeed, with not a single black face in sight.

Above the stalls from which the animals are released is a one-room announcer's stand. Since for every minute of action there are five minutes of preparation, the announcer becomes the central figure at the rodeo. It is he who must carry on a running monologue to maintain the spectators' interest in between events.

"Horse activities give the kids something to do," the announcer explains over the loudspeaker as a horseback drill team called Pegasus Patrol, consisting entirely of kids, fills the arena. "It keeps them busy." After a formidable display of well-regimented horsemanship, several young contestants try their hands at riding young bucking steers in the Junior Rodeo. Most fail. One of the boys is dressed up in full cowboy gear. "He's got his stirrups dug in and his gloves on and he looks like a little bitty shrunk-down version of the cowboys we'll see here later on today," announces the announcer. The kid looks disdainfully back over his shoulder as he walks away from his unsuccessful ride. The next contestant is a girl named Stacey. The announcer makes a joke or two about "female chauvinists." But Stacey manages to stay on top of her steer and winds up winning first place in her age group—beating out all the boys.

The kids are done and the serious competition is ready to begin. Most of the competing cowboys are professionals who follow the rodeos from town to town. They are members of Western Approved Rodeos, an organized league that gives points to the winners in each local event, keeps standings, and eventually crowns the "champions" of the year. But the cowboys are not like big-league ball players or other professional athletes in more lucrative sports. With the season half over, the top cowboys in the standings have won only $3,000. The all-time record for a year is $15,000, but most cowboys who follow the circuit might win only a thousand dollars or so. Considering the hardships and the costs (entry fees, horse care, travel expenses), it is more like an expensive hobby than a way to make a quick buck.

The excitement of the rodeo comes not so much from the competition between the cowboys themselves as from the competition between man and animal. The fans, of course, are partisans; they root for their own species. The crowd always cheers when a cowboy wins even if they've never heard of the chap. But the animals must be good, or the contest will be no fun. The horses, bulls, steers, and calves are thus all bred and raised especially for their spunk.

All the events involve either riding animals that buck or roping animals that are running away. In the bucking events, the

horses or bulls are released from their stalls after being electrically prodded and tied where they don't want to be tied. They
rear up and down, giving vent to their rage and trying to rid
themselves of their uncomfortable restrictions. The cowboys,
meanwhile, are expected to spur the animals on to even greater
antics while avoiding being thrown to the ground. By and large,
it's a rather even contest: sometimes the cowboys stay on, and
sometimes they do not. Roping, however, is more one-sided.
The cowboy ropes the fleeing calf around the neck. He quickly
dismounts his horse, throws the wailing calf to the ground, and
ties three legs in the air, leaving the calf totally paralyzed. The
calf registers strong vocal complaints, which are often an-
swered by the neighing of horses in the waiting pen nearby.

The competition between man and beast is keenest in an
event called bulldogging. Riding alongside a steer, a cowboy
must jump upon him from his horse while all three creatures are
in full motion. He must grab the steer by the horns, bring him to
a halt, and wrestle him to the ground. Since the steer weighs
three or four times as much as the man, this is no easy task.
When one of the wrestlers gets hurt, it's usually not the steer.
The cowboys in this event are always young and strong, as are
those in the various bucking contests. Only in calf roping do the
older cowboys get a chance to stay active in the rodeo.

All cowboys in all events start out wearing hats. More often
than not, the hats are blown off in the heat of the struggle. A
wayward hat, it appears, is a sign of dynamic action. Everybody
knows it is purely for show; everybody enjoys it nonetheless.

The performance of each cowboy is either timed or judged.
After the announcer gives the score for each event, he must fill
in the time until the next contestant is ready by telling jokes,
spinning yarns, or whatever. One of the favorites with this
crowd is the one about the Hell's Angels who poured water over
a truck driver's steak. When the story ends up with the driver
running his truck over the Hell's Angels, everybody cheers.
Truck drivers, in this particular assemblage of humanity, apparently rank second only to cowboys in prestige. Then there's the
one about the newlyweds. A bulldogging contestant has just
been married, which is all it takes to trigger the announcer off.

"Hope he has his strength back for this event," he remarks. "Bill says he never knew what happiness was until he got married, and by then it was too late." Then, while Bill is trying his hand at wrestling a steer, "This is the same problem he has at home. 'Yes, you will,' he says. 'No, I won't,' she says." The folks in the grandstand say that this announcer is one of the best they've had in years.

After the first day of the two-day rodeo, the people retire to their homes to eat, wash, relax, and prepare themselves for the annual Firemen's Ball. When the slick-looking country-and-western band starts playing all the old favorites at nine o'clock, however, the dance hall is still deserted. There are more people lingering outside the door than there are inside. Everyone, it seems, is waiting for someone else to come.

Slowly at first, and then with a sudden surge, the people arrive. There are dates and groups of stags, and a fair sampling of older married couples as well. Some of the women have on slacks while others are wearing fancy evening gowns and tossed hairdos. There seems to be some confusion as to whether this is a casual or a formal affair, yet everyone, in his own way, is neat and well groomed.

It is perfectly proper—indeed, even commendable—to act slightly drunk. That is what is expected of the occasion. People talk with poorly hidden enthusiasm about the fights that can be expected later on in the evening. Groups of young males commute from the dance hall to the parking lot in order to refuel. They take a certain pride in their staggering gaits, and in the random disposal of their beer cans into the bushes and the stream bed nearby.

The volunteer firemen, meanwhile, are too busy for that kind of thing: they are selling and collecting the tickets and tending the huge bonfire that has already been started in preparation for tomorrow's barbecue. Besides, they say, the dance is too rowdy for them. But is it really? No fights are reported, and the band rarely strikes up anything quicker than a fox trot. The youngsters, for their part, seem to feel that the dance is not quite rowdy enough.

Sometime in the wee hours of the morning, the night life

subsides and the last piece of wood is placed on the bonfire. By dawn there are no more flames and 1,550 pounds of choice beef are placed on the grill just above the coals. The concrete pit is then sealed with boards, canvas, and finally a layer of dirt.

At eleven o'clock sharp the pit is uncovered and the roasts retrieved with pitchforks. Everybody gets, quite literally, as much as he wants. The meat servers, all volunteer firemen, enjoy their task: they vie with each other to see who can give the most away, thrusting big hunks of juicy beef upon the waiting customers with obvious glee. The women, meanwhile, are placed in charge of the beans, potato salad, and rolls, while the kids hand out the paper plates and plastic spoons. But only the men can handle the meat, and only the men can serve the beer.

The second day of the rodeo is much like the first. The announcer repeats many of the same jokes, and the audience still laughs. The cowboys still circulate in the crowd, and the kids still perch upon the wooden chutes and mimic the behavior of their idols. They call each other "partner," just like the cowboys do; their dress, manner, and speech is all that of young cowboys-to-be. Yes, when they grow big and strong they too might join the rodeo. And so it is that the Wild West is preserved for future generations, long after the time when roping calves, wrestling steers, and riding wild horses were practical necessities of the open range.

The rodeo, in the words of an avid fan, is still "a way of life." Men who are too old to compete can still help with the stock, as can the kids who are yet too young. And men and boys of all ages aspire to the same set of values: to be manly, tough, witty, and able to drink when the situation arises. The women, in turn, are expected to admire these traits in their men—and to possess just a touch of toughness themselves.

Even here, however, in this last stronghold of Wild West culture, the automation of the twentieth century has left its mark. As the fans leave the stands, they jump into their shiny new cars and trucks. "This Here's Cowboy Country," reads the bumper sticker on a brand-new Lincoln. The parking lot comes alive with a gigantic symphony of motorized hums, whines, and roars. This is the people's reality, the animals just their hobby.

The kids might admire the cowboys, but unless they can drive and service their pickups they will never get anywhere in the ranching business these days. Repairing their vehicles will be a much more valuable skill than riding a bucking bronco, for it is mechanical know-how, not horsemanship, that is at a premium now. And how can they expect to follow the rodeo circuit if it's not in their motor vehicles?

Accompanying the Fortuna Rodeo is a traveling carnival: "Butler Amusements—The Cleanest Show in the West." There are shooting galleries and cotton-candy stands, rides that make you sick to your stomach and a couple of merry-go-rounds for the kids. But the merry-go-rounds aren't like they used to be just a few years past. Instead of riding horseback, the kids get to ride in replicas of dune buggies, motorcycles, and snowmobiles. And this at the rodeo!

"We are about to give away *free samples* of a *manufacturer's product*," announces a salesman on the midway of the Humboldt County Fair in Ferndale. His overly groomed hair and blue sports suit set him apart from the down-home folks who walk by his booth. On the velvet table in front of him his delicate fingers are stacking up neat little piles of fancy gold pen-and-pencil sets. People gather around, lured by the prospect of receiving, for free, some of these pretty artifacts of the modern-day world. "This is a new version of an old product, the only really *new* invention in a writing implement or instrument since the quill," the salesman says immodestly. He proceeds to demonstrate the "gravity lock" on the pen, which means that the pen point retracts automatically when it is held upside down. "This is a principle as old as the one that built the pyramids, but it is the first time it's been adopted to anything so small as a pen."

The gold pen-and-pencil sets, however, are not the "free samples" to be given away. Instead, what the salesman distributes to each eager spectator is one free cartridge apiece. He then proceeds to demonstrate yet another new product: a pen which hooks into a telephone and also functions as a letter opener and magnifying glass. The telephone pen (regularly $3.95) and the pen-and-pencil set (regularly $7.95) are being sold together for "only *two dollars*" (said boldly, with two fingers waving in the air) "and ninety-eight cents" (said softly, as if it were an afterthought). Actually, the salesman tells the crowd, they will be purchasing only the telephone pen and receiving the rest absolutely free—and that includes a special gold ink cartridge "which is not only gold, but this one is *perfumed*. Now that's something *really* new." He scribbles some lines on a piece of paper and passes it around; sure enough, it smells just like a synthetic flower.

When the salesman announces he can only "give away" gold gravity-lock pen-and-pencil sets to the first eight people purchasing telephone pens, people rush to the front waving their money. By now the $2.98 has been rounded off to an even three dollars, plus tax. Then, with the first round of sales completed, a *silver* pen-and-pencil set suddenly appears ("a $9.95 value," he claims) and the whole thing starts all over again.

This is no isolated event. Throughout the county fair, salespeople are demonstrating and peddling their water distillers, electric blenders, no-stick cookware, liquid embroidery, sewing machines, vacuum cleaners, encyclopedias, electric organs. Everyone, it seems, has something to push. A large trailer entitled "Energy and the Environment" turns out to be a Pacific Gas & Electric propaganda venture justifying its nuclear power plants and demonstrating that it cares about the environment by showing a picture of a transmission tower painted green. The Marines, meanwhile, continue their search "for a few good men."

The salesmen are all professionals who follow the country fair circuit. The pen vendor, aged forty-three, has been a drummer ever since he was eighteen years old. His sales pitch, repeated verbatim every hour or so, seems to have a will of its own which has little or nothing to do with the stone-faced man who delivers it. It's just a job like any other job, although it demands that he have no home other than the camper in which he travels. Like the barkers and peddlers of years past, the people of the fair are creatures of the road who remain forever on the outskirts of the communities they serve.

But the salesmen are not alone. The "carnies," as the amusement-park folks call themselves, have transformed the county-fair circuit into a way of life. Traveling together in one continuous party, they wear "carny power" insignia on the back of their Levi's jackets and like to hang together when the local toughs start hankering for a fight. They are proud to belong to a select group of "gypsies, tramps, and thieves," self-appointed outcasts from the small-town societies in which they set up shop. Like the salesmen who travel beside them, they live off the suckers ("Everyone loves being a sucker," a barker tells me authoritatively) who come to the fair to blow a few bucks and catch a passing glimpse of bright lights and fancy things.

Then there are the midway performers, professionals par excellence. The show is a small one, booked by an agency in Sacramento. The M.C., wearing slick, tight-fitting showman's clothes which reveal a good-sized paunch, announces with great fanfare that the first act is Bill Devon, a magician. Bill finds doves in empty handkerchiefs and makes cards appear from thin air. He is good: most of the time you can't see how it could possibly be done. But not great: sometimes you see a card in the back of his hand, or a dove slide down from his sleeve. Then there are the Kobelt Sisters, who do well-timed acrobatics in rag-doll costumes, then gradually strip down to virtually nothing as they continue to dance, play the xylophone and banjo, and do cartwheels in a jump rope. They have their act down pat; they should, for they have been practicing since they were kids—the same smiles, the same gestures, the same intonations thousands and thousands of times. Finally, there is Bernie Burns, or, as the M.C. calls him, "Mr. Personality Plus," who can play a harmonica while hiding it inside his mouth. Again, the act is impressive, but, as Bernie himself is the first to admit, "If it took some special talent or intelligence, I couldn't do it. It's just work, practice. You do it over and over until you get it down." And again, Bernie should know: he's been around for some twenty years now.

The entertainment is fun. Were we not already jaded by television, we would stand in awe at the practiced expertise of the performers. But by now we are all immune, for we have seen bigger and better acts hundreds of times before. The stars we see on TV can never make a mistake; they are totally beyond our reach. The performers here at the fair, by contrast, can and do make mistakes and are readily accessible to the audience. Bernie, the harmonica player, has been pretending he swallowed the harmonica. "It's in your mouth," a kid yells, as if to reveal the hidden secret. "Of course it's in my mouth," replies Bernie. "If it's down there"—he points to his stomach—"I wouldn't be alive to play it. But don't ruin my act."

County-fair horse racing, too, is a professional event. Professional stables enter their horses, which are ridden by professional jockeys. Seldom is there a local entry, and even less frequently a local winner. There are programs with past performances, betting booths, cold-beer stands, and the works. It is just like big-league racing, but in reality it is not: many of the races are for "maidens," horses who have never won a race in their class, while the others are for horses who have not won any races within the past year. If a horse gets too good, it is no longer eligible to run the county-fair circuit. The purses, accordingly, are only a fraction of those in big-time racing. But money is still bet freely, for this is the only time the horses ever race in Humboldt County.

The demonstration booths, the carnival, the entertainment, the races—these could be anywhere. The performers do the same acts in nightclubs, the salesmen demonstrate their wares in discount stores, while the horses run on other tracks. The cotton candy and hot dogs on a stick are the same as those sold throughout the country. It is over at the home-economics pavilion and inside the barns, however, that the local character and agrarian traditions of the county fair are preserved in perpetuity. Here, home-grown blood reigns supreme, as the 4-H clubs and women's groups—not the traveling professionals—are allowed to run the show. Homemade pies, home-canned fruit, home-knitted clothes, and home-grown vegetables are interspersed with miniature models of life on the farm. Well over half the entries bear ribbons; indeed, it is hard not to win a ribbon when so many of them are awarded. The competition is divided into literally thousands of "classes" and "sections," each one of which grants first-, second-, and third-place prizes. There is one section for apricot jam, and another for apricot-pineapple jam. There are 34 different types of cookie classifications and 118 categories for textiles (including seven separate pillow-slip sections and seven more for different types of towels). Flower arrangements can be entered in any one of 63 "themes" ("Indian Summer," "Country Music," "Way Out," etc.). Three ribbons are always available for each section, but three entries are not always present to receive them.

The judges are lenient. Rarely does an entry receive less than 90 out of 100 possible points; many wind up with a perfect score. Often, two first prizes are given in the same section. Sometimes categories appear from out of nowhere in order that an entry might win a prize. "Article by person over seventy-five years old" does not appear on the official list, but a ribbon is awarded nonetheless so that Grandma Jones can go home happy.

The barns, meanwhile, are teeming with life. Hundreds of sheep, swine, and cattle—each accompanied by a young owner from the 4-H Clubs or Future Farmers of America, who must keep his animal fed and groomed and his stall cleaned at all times—are mooing, baa-ing, and oinking simultaneously. This is no standard stable with barnyard flies and long lines of stock which all look alike. It is more like a party—for animals and people both. With hundreds of kids from all over the county spending the better part of a week in and around the three giant barns, the business of the fair is easily transformed into a major social occasion.

Fourteen-year-old Sarah is busily scurrying about as she cleans up after two young heifers. She is a 4-H Club member; her dad is not a farmer but a painting contractor; her mom is, "Well, you know . . . ."

"Do you stay here all the time during the fair?" I ask her.

"Yeah. It's kinda fun. It's something to do during the summer anyway."

"Have your heifers been judged yet?"

"No, tomorrow."

"What will they be judged on?"

"I don't really know."

"Then why are you entering them? What is special about them?"

"Well, they're mine."

"Is it really a big thing to win a ribbon?"

"It depends on how many animals you have. The Jacobis over there, well, for them it's not much because they have so many. But for me, I'd really like to win."

"Are you nervous about tomorrow?"

"Yeah," she says shyly, "kind of."

Just down the aisle, seventeen-year-old Vicki is comparing notes on the day's events with some friends who are perched on top of a bale of hay. Vicki, in her last eligible year with FFA, has already won six blue ribbons and three "champions" (a prize that crosses class lines—her heifer, for instance, beat out a mature cow for one of the awards). It is Vicki's big day, the highest moment of her youthful career. She has put a lot of energy into her fourteen sheep, thirty homing pigeons, dairy heifer, horse, and pony—and she is just now reaping the rewards. When I ask her if she wishes to own a farm someday, she replies quickly, "I want a ranch—*badly*." Then, with a deadly earnest frown, she adds, "But they cost a lot of money." Vicki is already on her way: she expects to show quite a profit when she sells her animals at the Junior Livestock Auction, and with the money she earns she will help put herself through college in agricultural science.

As the Saturday-night auction grows near, the mood of the fair begins to change. The kids will sell their animals and earn their profit—but they will also be parted forever from their barnyard companions. Susie Pritchard, a member of the Miranda 4-H Club, is gently carding the soft white wool on her ewe as she holds its black head to her breast. She has a long, sad face which is wet with tears.

"Will you be in the auction tonight?" I ask.

"Yeah," she says quietly.

"Will you miss your sheep?"

"Oh, yes!"

"It's her only one," explains her mother, who is standing

nearby. "We just don't have the space. . . . We'd like to keep her, but . . . but you have to be hardhearted to be a farmer. The idea is to make a profit, you know." Susie's mother, however, appears to be having some trouble herself in living up to her hardhearted advice.

But business, to some folks, is what the whole thing is about. The Bank of America has placed a large advertisement for the Junior Livestock Auction in the local paper: "These men and women will have raised their own animals, paid their own expenses, kept their own books. And they will all be experiencing the challenge of profit or loss in the management of their own business ventures. . . . Bank of America is proud to be part of the program. We finance many of these junior livestock projects." That is how it all works: the youngsters purchase animals from local farmers and ranchers, borrowing the necessary money from a bank or similar reputable sponsor; then, after the stock have been suitably raised, they are sold back to the local ranchers and businessmen, thence to be butchered and consumed. The sponsor thus plays a key role in the projects. "Getting acquainted with your banker," the FFA members are told in the official Project Guide, "is a valuable part of your training."

The auction itself is conducted with great fanfare. Real-life auctioneers volunteer their services, obviously getting quite a thrill from selling off sheep for as high as $6.50 a pound on the hoof, instead of the usual market price of forty or fifty cents. Tony Titus of Ferndale FFA is trying to sell his pig for a profit, and the auctioneer is there to see that Tony's pig commands a decent price. "Hundred-ninety-four-pounder. Boy, there's a choice hog right there, folks. There's a dandy. *Hey*, now-a-half-now-seventy-five-eighty-one-pick-up-the-one-seventy-five-and-now-eighty. Five. Now-eighty-five-and-now-ninety-now-ninety-five-five-*one*. Dollar-now-dollar-five-one-five-and-now-ten. One-fifteen. One-fifteen-one-twenty-one-fifteen-one-twenty-one-fifteen-here. Hey, pork chops went up, you know. One-twenty-one-twenty-five-hey-one-thirty. Now one-twenty-five-one-thirty-here-five-one-thirty-five. And now forty. And now five. And now fifty. And now . . ." Two of the five professional spotters have latched on to serious buyers willing to bid against each other. Their backs sweating, their eyes gleaming with maniacal zeal, the spotters whip their canes with lightning-swift movements when a buyer gives a nod of the head. The auctioneer, having started off at a feverish pace, now proceeds even quicker. "Now-five-sixty. One-sixty-one-sixty-five-dollar-seventy-five-seventy-one-seventy-five-and-now-eighty-one-seventy-five-eighty-one-seventy-five-and-now-eighty. *Hey,* one eighty. And now five. One-eighty-five-one-eighty-and-now-one-eighty-five-and-now-ninety. One ninety. Stop and think about it, that's awful cheap. One ninety. And now five. Don't you get balky," he says to one of the buyers. The spotter stares longingly into the eyes of his client, as if the world will come to an end if he chickens out now. The buyer, alas, finally buckles under the pressure and nods his head. "One-ninety-five-and-now-two. Two-dollar-bill. One-ninety-five-two-one-ninety-five-two. And now two. Are ya thinkin', sir? Two dollars. It's only money, tax deductible. Two dollars." The bidder looks questioningly toward his wife. "Don't talk to her, talk to me. One-ninety-five-and-now-two. Well, thank you anyway, I'm going to sell it. *Hey,* two dollars. Now-five-two-dollars-and-now-five-two-five. Now *he's* gonna get balky. Hey, two-dollars-here-five-two-here-five. Five? Two-oh-five? Two-oh-five? Thank you anyway, I sold it. Two-dollar-bill. Eureka Second Hand Exchange were the buyers. Thank you very much. You sure helped out. Every time you bid on these animals you help these kids with their education. And I'll tell you what, you very seldom see one of these boys, these farmer kids, in trouble. They're good kids."

Tony has been in the spotlight for scarcely a minute; his pig has been snorting in the straw underfoot even as his fate was being sealed. Tony quickly moves his animal out of the main ring and into the photographer's corner, where the oblivious swine continues to search the floor for food instead of posing for his picture. Four women scorekeepers, meanwhile, make the appropriate entries in their books (indeed, all the serious buyers in the audience mark down the final price and purchaser on their scorecards) while a crew of six FFA members proceeds to fill out and frame the plaque that will be presented within ten minutes to the Eureka Second Hand Exchange. And so it is that Tony Titus, like 181 other youngsters, undergoes his initiation into the cult of the professional ranchers. The kids experience both the pain and the profit of raising animals, and they are praised to the hilt by their elders for so gallantly taking up the torch.

County fairs are, or at least used to be, the backbone of rural American festivities. People used to come together at harvest time to share and compare their good fortunes—and to have fun. With the modernization of the overall texture of country living, however, the fairs themselves have changed. The bank has entered the livestock ring. The carnival has become mechanized, while employees of large companies have replaced independent shysters peddling their wares. Judging and award winning, once an adjunct to the proud displaying of crops, animals, and homemade articles, has become an activity in its own right. The standards of the judges, likewise, have changed with the times. All breads and cakes, for instance, are to be made with white flour. (Only one of the scores of baking categories is for "Whole Wheat," and even there up to three fourths of the flour used can be white.) And the taste is now for sweetness: the jams use as much sugar as fruit, and they are expected to stick like glue.

But through it all, a thread remains. It is still a place for down-home domesticity, and animals still reign over half the fairgrounds. The Girl Scouts offer free baby-sitting over by the main gate, while a boy leading a calf wanders innocently through the midway. And the sheer diversity of possible experiences at the fair keeps it alive as a summer festival. People still come in from all over the countryside, just as they did generations back when the fair was a place to see cows bigger than your own, cakes you could not possibly have baked yourself, fantastic inventions of all sorts, new cure-alls, and dazzling performers. Now, however, we've already seen the whole thing on

TV: from the acrobats and musicians on Ed Sullivan to the Betty Crocker cakes in the ads. And so, sadly enough, nothing amazes us quite the way it should.

Summer is a time for celebration, and every town, no matter how small, must find something to celebrate about. Fortuna has its Rodeo, Ferndale its County Fair. Willow Creek, having received national attention for the first time since the gold rush when a legendary half-human creature (called Bigfoot) was reportedly sighted in the nearby hills a few years back, naturally has its Bigfoot Days. Eureka, which must properly be called a city instead of a town since it is just a shade too big for everyone to know everyone else, is in a tizzy over the World Horseshoe Pitching Tournament. "For Eureka and surrounding Humboldt County, the World Championship competition marks the highest level of sporting activity ever to be held in the area," announces the lead article on the front page of the community newspaper. Miranda, on the other hand, is hardly more than a spot on the map, but it still manages to muster up enough energy for a yearly Bar-B-Que and Water Fight.

In Rio Dell (formerly Wildwood) the summer festival goes by the name of "Wildwood Days." "Oh, I just love Wildwood Days," says a young native. "Once a year the place just comes alive. People all dance in the streets. It doesn't matter what we do, I get out there and dance with my stepfather and we do steps I can't even begin to explain. But nobody cares. We all dance together. It's not like it is elsewhere, with the young people doing one thing and the old people something else."

This year, the town appears ready for the big event. Notices are posted everywhere, listing a jam-packed two-day schedule which will conclude with the first Log-o-rama ever to be held in Rio Dell. The store windows are painted with cartoon cowboys and 49'ers and old-time loggers eating beans.

The first event, according to the signs, is a parade to be held at eleven o'clock on Saturday morning. At ten-thirty I see no indications of anything but the usual traffic along Highway 101, which is the main street of town.

"Where's the parade going to be?" I ask the men in the barbershop.

"I don't know," says the barber. "Hey, Jack, is that parade today?"

"Yeah, I think so."

"Where is it?"

"I guess it'll come right down here somewhere." It's a reasonable assumption, since there's only one street in downtown Rio Dell.

Soon glimmerings of music filter through the motorized drone of the cars and trucks. A loudspeaker has been set up across the street and a set of square dancers, ranging in age from fifteen to fifty-five, is performing on the sidewalk. A small crowd begins to form to check out the action. The people are not nearly as primed, or as numerous, as the crowd at the rodeo parade in Fortuna. The snappy western gear found at the rodeo is lacking here, for these are not horse lovers and cowboys but simple working people whose lives are centered on the huge mill located in nearby Scotia. The men's bodies appear bent by their jobs. Many of the women have their hair in curlers, while those whose curlers have been removed display hairdos that rise in conspicuous consumption of stay-at-home care and attention.

The square dancing stops. A man looks at his watch. "Well, it's already eleven o'clock and it hasn't started yet." The sound system is playing "Anchors Aweigh," not because Rio Dell has any particular association with the Navy, but because the song happens to appear on a ten-year-old record of "Military Marches" that somebody has determined to be appropriate parade-type music. Two lanes of the four-lane highway have been blocked off, but the traffic continues to speed by on the remainder of the thoroughfare.

Finally, a police siren wails and the parade is under way. There are scarcely a dozen entries, highlighted by a woman in an evening gown with a sign saying "Madam X," several members of the Ladies' Auxiliary dressed in working clothes and mustaches, and, bringing up the rear, a hangman. The whole parade is over in about five minutes.

"Is that the end?" asks a bystander.

"It was better last year," remarks another.

The street, however, has been reserved for an hour, so when the parade reaches the far end of town it doubles back for a repeat performance. This time a white Valiant inhabited by an unsuspecting family somehow gets trapped in the line by mistake. Nobody seems to notice, including the driver. When the parade comes to a halt near the sound truck, the Valiant finally catches on and disappears. Some teen-age girls, meanwhile, pick up the idea and inconspicuously join the show in a car with an old "Impeach Nixon" sign hanging on the side.

The awards are given: "In dune-buggy class, first place goes to . . . the dune buggy!" And so on. When the hour is over, everyone leaves.

"What did you think of the parade?" I ask an old man with a cane.

"Oh, that was a dandy, wasn't it?" he says enthusiastically. Then, as an afterthought, "But it wasn't very long."

Up at the Firemen's Park, the "Arcade" has supposedly opened and the "Games" are scheduled to begin. "What's up there?" I ask a worldly-wise adolescent girl, self-consciously wearing eye shadow, who is walking away from the park.

"Oh, it's nothing."

"You mean it's all over?"

"No, there's nothing there."

I assume she is just belittling the insignificant carryings-on of her home town, but in fact she is telling the truth: nothing is happening up at the park. Nobody seems to know why the games are not being held. The signs had proudly announced there would be "greased pig, ladies' nail driving, rolling-pin throw, three-legged race, water-balloon throwing. Many more. Ribbons awarded." And so people are waiting around, but the games never start.

The "Arcade" itself is strictly a local operation. There are neither rides, cotton-candy stands, nor professional carnival booths with their giant kewpie dolls seducing the innocent country folks to try their luck at games they will never win. Instead, there are only counters of homemade pastries, sand-

wiches, and chili served up by women from the Degree of Poca-
hontas 119, the Horseshoe Club, and the American Legion
Auxiliary, and by young girls from the Christian Youth Organization. There are two booths featuring games of skill, both run
by Lions Club members dressed in straw hats and silly clothes
and giving poor imitations of real-life barkers. The prizes they
give away—three-foot plastic canes, rubber funny men, and, for
repeat winners, miniature stuffed animals which are replicas of
those which can be won at real-life carnivals—are not worth the
cost of playing the games. Nevertheless, it is at the stand with
the cork-shooting guns that the biggest crowd has gathered: a
dozen or so boys are obsessed with the possibility of making
eighteen consecutive hits and winning a tiny stuffed animal, or
perhaps just with the chance of proving their manliness by their
marksmanship.

Up at the Volunteer Fire Department's beer stand, a group
of young men are passing the time with small talk of pro football, cars, and the mill. They all work for the nearby Pacific
Lumber Company, and most of them grew up together here in
town. As the day wears on and the rest of the crowd gradually
begins to thin out due to the lack of stimulating activities, the
beer drinkers become more and more relaxed. The booth is soon
transformed into an ad hoc game of hit-the-cups-off-the-board-
with-a-ball. When somebody wins, a round of drinks is ordered
on the house and the rules of the game are changed. Friendly
jive talk slowly gives way to more rowdy behavior, culminating
in a cake being splashed over someone's head. From here it's
downtown to the bars, which in turn leads to playing football
on the sidewalks and having water fights with beer.

Wildwood Days has now begun in earnest. The parade, the
arcade, the games that never were—these, it turns out, were
mostly just for show. Nobody ever takes them very seriously.
What really counts is just to have one hell-of-a-good-time on
Saturday night. "It's the only time of the year you can drink in
the streets," says one of the young men, who happens to be
drinking in the streets. "Once a year it's a lot of fun."

"This is what we live for," adds another of the millworkers.

"To party every weekend." And Wildwood Days is the grandest party of them all.

By sundown the band has begun playing on a downtown street corner. They play a standard assortment of country-and-western tunes, with both a slow and a fast version of each one in order to double their repertoire. "Sounds like a funeral march," says an adolescent who is accustomed to more lively fare than the Johnny Cash-looking musicians have to offer. The kids break into laughter when the band strikes up with "We don't smoke marijuana in Muskogee . . ." Apparently, in this Muskogee, they do.

But nobody really cares if the band is good or bad. It's music and it's loud, and that's what counts. Everybody dances with anybody, just like I was told: sons with mothers, fathers with daughters, dates with each other. All sizes, sexes, shapes, and ages are moving with the music in a random assortment of steps and bodily contortions. And it's not just here on this one corner, but all over town. Each of the three "clubs" is jam-packed and overflowing; one of them features another band—a younger one with a livelier beat. The sidewalks are lined with roving gangs of teen-agers too young to get into the clubs. They play cops and robbers with the town's small police force, which consists of two men and a woman who are circulating through the crowds as if they were at a cocktail party. But the cops aren't very serious about their end of the game. "Just don't let us see it" is their general attitude. Minors are expected, perhaps even encouraged, to drink—if only just this once. The law is temporarily suspended for Wildwood Days as a year's worth of restrictions, inhibitions, and repressions of small-town life are all abandoned. "Once a year," as they say, "the place just comes alive."

Just as drunken behavior is expected on Saturday night, so is a hangover on Sunday morning. People speak with pride about how lousy they feel. By noon, however, the festivities are resumed with the annual spaghetti feed and raffle. The first prize: one half a beef, the ultimate symbol of affluence in this working class, family-oriented community. When the winner turns out to be the fire chief, one lady remarks: "He doesn't need it. Why doesn't one of us poor slobs who hasn't eaten meat for months get it?"

Finally, it's time for the featured event: Rio Dell's first annual Log-o-rama. But the logging contest starts off in true form: they can't get the logs into the Little League ball park until somebody decides to remove the fence. A forklift is called in, and the fence is pulled from the ground. A truckload of logs, supplied by the Pacific Lumber Company, is dumped on the field.

The Log-o-rama might be new to Rio Dell, but its competitive events, such as ax throwing, choke setting, and hand bucking, constitute a well-established sport in the logging country of the Northwest. Loggers who work during the week take off on weekends to follow the contests from town to town. The Lumberjack Association, which crowns the state champion, keeps a record of who has won each event. The logging games here in Rio Dell, however, do not have official standing with the Association, so this time it's just for fun.

A thirty-three-year-old man named John Clark, it turns out, has single-handedly put the show together. John is in a close three-way race for the state championship in hand chopping, but he has taken time out to stage the event in Rio Dell just because he loves the sport so much. He is built like the old-time loggers who used to pose for pictures beside their fifteen-foot stumps, with his striped suspenders holding his pants high above his waist and his muscles bulging out from under his red T shirt. His left hand and wrist, however, are wrapped in a monstrous bandage. "I got tangled up with my daughter in a crosscut," he says. "Thirty stitches worth." It happened only yesterday, he tells me, during a championship event over in Grass Valley. The injury might slow him down, but it would take more than thirty stitches to keep John Clark from competition.

"John never has a bad word to say with anybody," says John's teen-age nephew, who is helping to set up the target for the ax throwing. "He's really a nice guy."

"He looks like quite a logger," I add.

"Oh, yes," the boy says with pride. "Once he set the record for logs felled and bucked in one day. I think it was 177."

(Later, I ask John if it's true: "Did you really fell and buck

177 logs in a day?" "A hundred and ninety," he says, "in seven hours. But," he adds modestly, "that was under ideal conditions.")

A crowd has now gathered: perhaps three hundred people seated casually on the grassy hillsides which border the Little League field. There is no admission charge. The announcer, of course, is John Clark, who uses a bullhorn to tell the spectators which company each of the contestants works for.

The first event is ax throwing. A can of beer is placed in the center of the target, so there can be no doubt when somebody hits the bull's-eye. The function of the beer, however, is symbolic as well as practical: even the kids in the crowd are wearing Budweiser T shirts. "Let's see some beer," the spectators yell in encouragement. "Hit it!"

When it's John Clark's turn to compete, he hands the bullhorn to someone else and proceeds to excite the fans with his highly unorthodox one-handed delivery. But the ax fails to stick in the target. It is the last event of the day that John will fail to win.

Choke setting comes next. The contestant must jump over a half dozen logs before setting choke, and then return to his starting position. This is really just an obstacle course, but the biggest applause of the day comes when one of the participants turns out to be too drunk to stay on his feet. "No contestant will be permitted to compete while under the influence of alcohol," say the rules. But nobody really cares; after all, this is still Wildwood Days.

In hand chopping and hand bucking, John Clark is unexcelled. His time for chopping is half that of his closest opponent. He gives friendly encouragement and useful advice to the younger competitors who lack the professional skill that comes with age, but all his coaching is to no avail: he can hardly help but win himself.

The chain-sawing event draws loud cheers because the logs are cut so quickly. The "Jack and Jill" bucking is a favorite for its family appeal. (The winners, of course, are John and Rita Clark.) But the day's climax comes with a giant tug-of-war, although it isn't until the last minute, and not before several urgent appeals through the bullhorn, that two teams are formed.

After the games, Rita Clark tries to fit eight huge trophies into a cardboard box.

"Where will you put them?" I ask.

"Oh, everywhere," she says. "They pretty much fill the house up."

The crowd disperses, and Wildwood Days is over. Like Christmas, it comes but once a year. The citizens of Rio Dell will have to wait for 364 days until they are once again permitted to drink in the streets.

The Pacific Lumber Company, meanwhile, retrieves the logs that have not been cut up. They have no use, however, for the short rounds of wood which are left on the field.

"Say, John," I ask the champion, "can we have some of that wood for our stove?"

"Sure," he says with a grin. "You want me to chop it for you?"

Here, I say to myself, is a man who still loves his work, a master craftsman who is proud of his trade. Just as the cowboys at the rodeo uphold the culture of the open range, men like John Clark ensure that good woodsmanship will not be lost forever. Of course, throwing an ax at a tree is no more useful today than riding a bucking bull. But it's the thought that counts, the idea that there is something in these pioneer traditions that is worthy of being preserved.

Part Three
OLD FOLKS

And even if I do get better, I'm too old to work.
So what good is it? Tell me that—
what's the use if you're too old to work?

—GLEN STRAWN

———————————————

6

The Death and Life
of Old Glen Strawn

GLEN, AGED EIGHTY-ONE, shared one half of a small duplex in town with his second wife, Amy. Outside the murky green structure was a sitting porch which was rarely sat upon; inside, the place was furnished with only the bare necessities. There were only a few of those memorial knickknacks which adorn the homes of so many elderly folks. The kitchen showed little sign of use; the living room was kept neat and tidy primarily because there was never much going on to mess it up. The apartment was most definitely rented: a place where Glen and Amy passed their time, a transition between the constant activity of life out in the woods and . . . well, and that truly passive state which loomed ahead on the not too distant horizon.

Glen spent the better part of his days sitting upright in a sturdy easy chair, an electric light shining over his shoulder. His can of tobacco would be perched on one arm of the chair and an ashtray on the other as he plowed his way through one paperback Western after another. "Beats TV," he'd say apologetically. "But, Christ, most of these fellas can't write worth a damn. Lotta fights and shootin', but that's about it."

Glen, like many old-timers, loved to talk, and his mind was startlingly clear. But he didn't get around much any more; my invitations for him to come visiting my cabin out in the woods were all politely declined. At best, he'd chop up his firewood (several cords neatly stacked outside) and hand-sharpen his saws. One day I showed up with my two dull crosscuts, hoping to learn his skill. But I had come too late: Glen had just been taken to the local hospital for the second time in as many months. First it was a broken hip, and now something with his lungs.

"I'd like to see Glen Strawn," I told the woman at the hospital desk.

"Are you related?"

"No, just friends." A puzzled look came across the receptionist's face as she no doubt wondered how a young man and an octogenarian could be "just friends." Reluctantly, perhaps even suspiciously, she directed me to his room.

I found Glen half slumped over in a wheelchair, sporting a week-old beard. "Well, Ray," he said in his deep, gruff voice, which resonated in several tones at once. "I was just thinking you might stop by. How was your trip? When did you get back?"

"Oh, it was okay."

"Back East, wasn't it? Wasn't it your folks you got back there?"

"Yeah, my folks. But I hear you've been through some hard times."

"Christ, Ray, you wouldn't believe it. It's been hell. They had me up in Eureka somewheres and wouldn't let me go. Hell of an operation they got up there. Feels like it's been years. When was it you left?"

"January."

"Is that all? Feels like . . ." There was a commotion in the hallway. Amy, accompanied by several nurses and the ambulance driver, stormed into the room.

"Oh, they're going to take you away," she exclaimed. "But I'll be right there with you, I promise I will. Joan will drive me up today and I'll stay with you just like I did before."

"Don't be in such a hurry," said Glen. "Nobody's going anywhere, far as I know."

"Oh, yes, you are. You have to go to Eureka. They don't have the machinery down here. But I'll . . ."

"No, I'm not," he announced. "I'm going home."

"No, Glen, you have to go to the General Hospital in Eureka," said one of the nurses. "We aren't set up for intensive care here, so you have to go there. They'll take good care of you, I promise."

But Glen had been there before. "That rat trap?" he growled. "Hell, no. I'm going home."

They handed him a release form to sign. He received the piece of paper courteously and pretended to glance it over, although he was without his glasses and therefore couldn't read. "Well, there's lots to be considered before you can come to a decision in a matter like this," he said philosophically. "We can't just be jumping to any conclusions."

"Here," said Amy. "I'll sign it."

"It's a scandal," Glen said.

But nobody was listening to him any more. With the paper signed, they all proceeded in a businesslike manner to get everything ready for the journey. "I tell you, it's a scandal," he continued. "I seen it with my own eyes. They were right here in this room. All of them. They're all the same, each one as bad as the next."

A nurse looked at me with a knowing glance. "He's senile," she said with her eyes. "Just chatter. We adults of course know better."

Glen rambled on. "But it's nothing new. It goes way back to Teapot Dome, and even before that. Politicians been doing it all along. Right here in this room I seen it. Talking like they don't know a thing, but everyone knows they done it. It's written all over their faces." Senile? Idle chatter? It seemed obvious to me that Glen had been watching the Watergate hearings on TV and had registered definite concern. Perhaps he compared the messed-up state of the nation to his own unfortunate condition.

Still talking, Glen was maneuvered onto a stretcher. "I'm sorry this had to happen right now," he told me from his prone position, "before we even had a chance to chat." They rolled him out of the room.

When I arrived at the geriatric ward of Eureka's General Hospital later in the week, I found Glen sound asleep. He was huddled under his covers, white as a sheet. The nurse explained they had just put him down with a strong dose of tranquilizers: he had been up all night and had apparently kept the rest of the ward up with him by his boisterous carryings-on.

Glen finally awoke several hours later, gazing about with a startled, blank stare. He noticed there was a person in his room, but did not appear to recognize who it was. "I'm Ray," I said.

"I know you're Ray," he responded matter-of-factly, "but that doesn't answer my question. Where am I?"

"In Eureka."

"Well, what am I doing here?"

"You're sick. You're in the General Hospital in Eureka until you get better."

"What's wrong with me?" He was still trying to get his bearings.

"That's what they're trying to find out."

"Well, why don't they hurry up with it? They oughta know by now. Why can't I get better at home?"

"They have special machines up here."

"Yeah, I can hear them now. Listen." We listened together, but to no avail.

"I can't hear them," I finally admitted.

"Listen. Out there." He pointed to the window. What I heard was the traffic outside.

"Those are cars," I explained.

"Well, where are they all going?" Glen was not used to the sounds of city life.

"Just here and there."

"You'd think they woulda got where they were going by now. You know, I'm glad you came, Ray. I was hoping you could help me. I can't quite get my fingers on it. Do you know what it is?"

"What what is?" I asked.

"What it's all about. Why I'm here. What's going to happen. What's the answer. What's the reason for it all. Can you tell me, Ray? Can you tell me what the answer is?" There was a sense of urgency in his request. I knew what he was talking about now:

he was concerned with the basic question of life and death. But I didn't know how to help him. He was being very direct, too direct for my own comfort. His blue-gray eyes met mine straight on with a piercing intensity. I tried to avert my glance, but found myself unable to do so. I thought of glib responses to his question but could not manage to pronounce them.

"I don't know, Glen. That's what we all would like to know."

"Sometimes I think I almost have it, it's right at my fingertips, but then it just slips away. Maybe I'm going crazy."

"No, you're not going crazy."

"Then why can't I remember anything? I try to catch hold of something and I just can't hang on to it. I must be going crazy. I can't tell what's true any more or what I'm just dreaming." There was a note of desperation in his voice.

"Really, Glen," I assured him, "you're not going crazy. It's just a physical problem. Your lungs aren't pumping enough oxygen to your brain, so you're having trouble with your memory. They told me they know that much."

"I don't wanna be crazy," he said.

"As soon as your lungs get a little better, you'll be able to remember everything." I tried to sound convincing, but it was hard. We both suspected that his lungs were not about to turn right around and get better at this late stage.

"What do you think is going to happen now?" he asked.

"You'll stay here till you get better and then you'll go home."

"No, I don't know what I'll do. Looks like this is the end of the road."

"I don't know about that. You're tough." And he was. Glen was definitely a fighter.

"No, I'm not, Ray. They took it all out of me. I'm not tough any more. Right here in this hospital, they did me in. I'm just like a baby. I can't even take care of myself. Can't even go to the bathroom. They got me hooked up with all these bedpans and things. Hell of an outfit they got here. Here, help me up a bit." I cranked on the foot of his bed, raising him halfway to a sitting position. "And even if I do get better, I'm too old to work. So what good is it? Tell me that—what's the use if you're too old to work?"

Right then the nurse came in. "Oh, you're just imagining things, Glen," she said with a smile. "Nothing's the matter." Perhaps working in the geriatric ward necessitated such an attitude, but it rang false in my ears. Here was a man seriously grappling with the problem of his own imminent death, and she dismissed it all with an affected grin. It seemed like Glen deserved more attention than that.

"Here's your pills," she said in a tone generally reserved for children. "Now be good and take your pills."

"What are they?" Glen asked.

The nurse hemmed and hawed.

"Well, we'll have to see about this," Glen said with his philosophic air. "There's lots of considering to be done in matters like this."

The nurse quickly put an end to such nonsense. "If you don't take the pills, we'll have to come in and give you injections." Glen took the pills.

After the nurse left, Glen started telling stories. He told of his journey to the Orient as a youth. His buddy was taking up with a young woman in the Philippines. The girl, as it turned out, had a boy friend, who drew a knife on his rival, Glen's pal. But Glen was right there on the scene, and he raised a chair over the attacker's head. It was a wrought-iron chair, the kind usually found in old-fashioned ice-cream parlors. For the next half hour, Glen engaged in a digression on the manufacture, use, and history of wrought-iron chairs. He told everything he knew about them, and that was a lot: somehow, somewhere along the line, Glen had become an expert on the matter. It seemed that the story about the Philippines had been forgotten, and I was left hanging with knife drawn and chair uplifted. But in the end Glen's memory held out, and he returned to his original tale: he finally lowered the boom on his buddy's rival, the fellow with the knife, and then had to jump ship to escape punishment. We spent another half hour on board an English vessel and prancing around various seaports in India.

As the afternoon wore on, Glen began to show signs of fatigue. I told him I should be leaving. "Don't go," he pleaded. "Don't leave me." I told him I'd come back, but for now . . . "No, please don't leave," he insisted. He was almost in tears. For the past two hours, he had been in contact with the world; left alone, he knew he would fade away into the abyss of his own non-memory, where he couldn't quite put his finger on anything—or even know what it was he was trying to put his finger on in the first place.

Glen was engaged in a head-on battle with his own senility— that was what he feared most and fought hardest against. For one afternoon, at least, he had won. With someone to take him seriously, to listen to him respectfully, he could still exercise his brain with remarkable clarity and dexterity. The professional staff at the hospital would hardly have believed it, for it was obvious from my talks with them that they regarded Glen as nothing short of a raving maniac, with neither rhyme nor reason to his ramblings. And they treated him accordingly.

A week or two later, with Glen stubbornly refusing to die and his body stubbornly refusing to get any better, he was transferred to the Sea View Convalescent Home. The atmosphere there was much like that of the geriatric ward: a few groans coming from the rooms, a few adventuresome souls struggling with walkers in the long, sterile corridors, but for the most part just people who were far too old to do anything more strenuous than simply sit up.

I started my first visit to Glen's new home with talk of the weather, as sounds from the hallway filtered into the room. "Did you hear that shot?" Glen asked. It was a door slamming. "There it goes again. Must have nabbed him by now." We heard the casual murmuring of voices outside. "They're coming up with a decision now," Glen pronounced with great concern. What it was they were deciding he did not say. "But what I want to know is who's paying for all this? This hospital outfit ain't doing it for free. Who's taking care of the money? It must be all gone by now." Glen always was a very practical fellow.

A new nurse came in and introduced herself. Her name was the same as someone he used to know years ago down by Briceland. He assumed it was the same person, despite an obvious discrepancy in age. After the nurse left, he spent a long time talking about her. In his mind, his lost friend had come alive. As he had feared during our last visit, he could no longer distinguish between dream and reality. His world was inside himself.

Glen asked me to rub his shoulder, which I did. It felt strange: he was, quite literally, all skin and bones. He took my hand and held it. "We're partners," he said. "You and I have come a long way together. It's been a tough fight, but we made it through. They said we couldn't, but we showed 'em anyway." He squeezed on my hand. "Partners to the end, eh, Ray? It's been a long hard road, but . . . What's that? There it goes again. More shots. Christ, what do you reckon they're after? Quail?" My hand was still in his; in the culture that Glen came from, men never held hands.

"I think it's just a door slamming."

"Sounds mighty loud for that. Sounds more like shots to me. Quail or rabbits, one or the other."

"I brought the article," I said.

"You did? You have it here?" I reached in my bag for the copy of *Clear Creek* magazine, opening it to the page with the picture of Glen and his gentle smile. "Sure enough, that's me. And the whole story is true, too. Every last word."

The true story of Glen's life is packed with action and variety, but it is firmly based on a rural lifestyle. "We was on a homestead when I was young," Glen recalled in his magazine article.

Hell of a life. Christ, we'd never see nobody for months. It wasn't too well settled in that country at that time. Back in the '90s, you know. It was twelve miles to town, and I had to go to town once a week. That's a twenty-four-mile ride on horseback. Got the mail, and took a weekly paper. Had to get that weekly paper. It was 1897 when I can really remember it. The Spanish-American War was agoing on, and also the Gold Strike in the Yukon was on. They was all excited about the war. I didn't give a damn about the war, the Yukon was what I was interested in. . . .

But that was a great life for a kid. I killed deer when I was seven years old. With a rifle. It was pretty near a must: if you wanted some meat to eat, you had to go kill a deer, or else kill a critter. I was a tough little kid, let me tell you. Sometimes it was catch a jackrabbit or no breakfast. Didn't butcher our cattle much. No way to keep it, except only jerk it. Sometimes there'd be three or four families, and then we'd butcher one. Each take a part of it, and get along pretty good that way. . . .

And we put in . . . oh, probably six months in the mountains every year. Hair clear down to here when we came back. Up in the mountains, we had to guard the stock from bears and cats. Our dogs would tree the cats, then we'd come by and shoot them. Bears were a big problem. Bear would come by and chase a whole herd of sheep and gulch them: the sheep would run into a gulley faster than they could get out. Sheep'd just pile up and smother themselves. So we'd hunt the bear and eat the meat. We didn't know nothing of that trichina bug. Made mighty good jerky. You take a bear and skin him, though, and he looks almost human.

When we was up in the mountains, me and the old man built ourselves a log cabin. I was just a kid and old Ferrerra he done all the hard work, you know. I just went along and . . . well, I was only seven years old. Of course, I was a lot of help to him because he couldn't get around and I could. So building the cabin, we went up in the timber and cut the poles and then I had a mule and I'd sled them down and set the long ones on the sides of the cabin and the short ones across the ends. We cut them and peeled them first, then he measured them off and notched them and then we rolled them up. As soon as it got too high, we put up skids. Put the rope around the logs and then pulled up with the mule when it got too high for us. We couldn't lift them—they was too heavy—so we pulled them up with the mule.

We went and cut down a big sugar pine and made the shakes—they was about thirty inches long—and put the roof on. Chinked it all up with mud and moss. Took the moss off the trees and made a muck out of it. When you put the poles up, you lay the moss in there and that stops the breeze from going through—a lot anyways.

Glen left home at a tender age and signed up on a transport ship packing suitcases for the officers. By the time he was fourteen he had already been to the Orient and back. Upon his return he went back into the woods to work as a teamster during the tanbark boom. He worked eighteen hours a day, six days a week: "You didn't hardly sleep—might as well trade your blankets off for a lantern." He worked with both horses and mules, but he always preferred mules:

Had one pack mule followed me everywhere I went—no rope or nothing. We'd drive ten, twelve head of mule with just one line. Jerk that line and say, "Gee, gee." Line is attached to the leader, and when he feels that pull he turns. The teams had all these hames, the ones with the bells on 'em, and they'd be ringing in time with the steps. You'd hear the other fella's bells acomin', and you'd pull off to the side soon as you could. Then they started coming in with automobiles on the wagon roads. We used to spend most of our time back in those days leading horses and mules past them automobiles.

Being a man of some ambition, Glen saved up his money and invested it all in a rice farm in the Sacramento Valley. Storms ruined his first crop, however, and he went bankrupt. From then on it was just one thing after another as Glen sought his way in the world of affairs:

After the rice I went to shooting ducks for the market. Me and two other fellas. I made five thousand dollars in two months shooting ducks. Sell 'em in San Francisco. Take a load of ducks down and bring a load of whiskey back. Get 'em coming and going.

I put in eighteen months down in South America after that—Peru. Building a railroad across the top of that wild rubber forest. On the west coast of South America, there's wild rubber forests in there. Thousands and thousands of acres. We worked for an English outfit. Twelve and a half thousand feet up, that railroad was.

I been to Guatemala, too. I met a guy who had a contract with Folger's Coffee Company. We was gonna fly that coffee from inland out to the ocean where they can get it on the boats. They used to pack it out; Christ, it would take them three weeks to pack a load out from them plantations. We was gonna make an airport out there. This fella was a good aviator, but he got to barnstorming—looping the loop, and he never did come out of it. Stuck it in the ground. Whatever happened, I don't know. That's what raised hell with our contract. That stopped it, 'cause I didn't fly myself. . . .

Later on we used to fish out of Shelter Cove. I fished two years for the market. During Prohibition, so I hauled whiskey most of the time. Made lots of money hauling whiskey. Three or four boats laying out there twenty-five miles—you just go out, get a load, and bring her in. They had big stills working on the boat. Label it "Canadian Whiskey." They had labels for everything—any kind you want. Go out there and bring it in—it was a cinch you could sell it. Went down one time and got a load of tequila. Nine dollars a case down there, brought it up and sold it for ninety-six dollars a case. Four days and four nights on board ship. That was good times then. When I was gonna go out and get a load of whiskey, I'd fish all day with no hooks on the line—just go round and round. Finally I was the last boat, I'd go out to the mother ship, get a load of whiskey and come on in. Wouldn't even tell my brother when I was gonna do it. Them hijackers was pretty bad. They get you and knock you in the head and take your load of whiskey and scuttle your boat and sink it. They was dangerous. I wasn't scared of the Revenue—it was them hijackers I was scared of, 'cause they kill you for a load of whiskey. We had a Lewis machine gun—when we'd get a load, we'd always set her up. We never had to use it, but we always had it set up.

During the Depression I had a sheep ranch. Couldn't sell no wool, but I just stored it and after the Depression was over, I sold it. It was thirty-five cents a pound and in two months it went to six bits a pound—after I had held it for three years. And I worked for the Forest Service, too. Built lots of roads for them when they had the C.C.C. camps.

I worked for W. P. Fuller, the paint man. Used to go out with his boy—taught him how to hunt and fish. Give me ten dollars a day for that. All during school vacation, I was with the kid.

And I had lots of hunters, policemen mostly, would come up from Oakland and San Francisco to my place to go hunting. I had eighteen head of horses; I could pack them anywhere. Or kill them a buck if I had to. They'd come up and stay with me for a week or two on their vacation, and, hell, I'd get a hundred dollars apiece out of them before they got away. No, I never felt the Depression.

That was a good deal up there. The sheep were more or less velvet to me. Oh, you had to take care of them. The old lady stayed on the ranch most of the time, and I had a couple of nephews stay with her, and they took care of the sheep. One year there came a big snow. I always was prepared for it—had lots of hay and grain, you know. Five foot of snow. If I hadn't had a barn full of hay, I'd have been out of the sheep business that year. But I brought 'em through. Raised ninety percent lambs, too. Lambed in January, five below zero. Son of a bitch, if that wasn't a winter! I worked one shift and the old lady worked the other; I worked the night shift and she worked the day shift when we was lambing. You had to be right there because the lamb would freeze that quick. I raised the barn up seven feet, put a false floor in, and when I put the hay in I put it on top of that. I had my lambing shed underneath all that hay. Then when the snow banked up around the barn, why, it was warm as toast in there. But between there and the house it wasn't warm, by a hell of a lot. Chopped wood to keep the old fireplace going.

It was thirty miles to a store. When the snow got on top of the mountains, you didn't get out 'til spring. We was three thousand feet up. Buy groceries twice a year, spring and fall.

During the winter, I'd trap. One winter my brother and I trapped and we had eight hundred dollars' worth of fur in the spring. Foxes, cats, 'coons, mink, fisher, mountain lion, bear, everything. Of course, the bear hibernate 'long about the first of December, and you don't see any more of them 'til spring. They're just about coming out now. A few sunshiny days in April, that brings them out.

In those days, it was all pack trails. There was no roads way up there at all. That's what I had all those horses for—to pack these hunters. Pack their game out and pack their whiskey and provisions in: they always had a few provisions, but mostly whiskey. During Prohibition, they had their own bootlegger used to come up there with them. Cops, from Oakland. They sure had it fixed.

It was all right, I guess. At the time it was all right. But I just got tired of being out in that brush. Why, sometimes it'd be three, four months before you ever saw anybody.

Glen finally sold off his sheep ranch and went to work for the railroad in Mendocino County. From there he got into logging. "I'd run loading machine, run the Cat, run locomotive. Everything. I built all them roads for years—all up and down the Mattole and where you turn off up by China Creek—I built all them logging roads. Wore out three Cats. All new Cats, too, to start with." He kept working in the woods as long as he was physically fit to do so.

"Guess I done most everything," he concluded. "Doesn't seem like much, though, just one thing after the other. There's a lot to do out here."

"This is proof," said Glen as he waved the magazine in his hand. "This proves what I've been saying all along." What it proved was that his life had amounted to something after all, that he was a person who really *mattered*. It was all written out and published for everyone to read. He was more than just a senile old man waiting out his days in a rest home—he was Glen Strawn the teamster, the rice farmer, the bootlegger, the rancher, the logger. He was a man who had been around, a man of the woods and the world—however feeble he appeared to be just then. As I left, Glen was proudly displaying the magazine in front of him, wearing a grin as wide as his face. "I'll hold it up here so they all can see it soon as they come in," he said.

How strange, I thought, that Glen's life needed "proof"—but apparently it did.

When I returned a couple of weeks later, the receptionist told me, after checking the register, that no one by the name of Glen Strawn was presently there. Was he sent back to the hospital, or released to go home? No, he wasn't on the transfer list either. But there in the Daily Census Book, under the column entitled "Expiration Dates," was Glen Strawn's name. "I'm afraid he's expired," she said in a quiet, concerned voice. "He's dead," I repeated to myself. The word "expired" somehow seemed too polite.

The context of Glen's death was totally out of kilter with that of his life. A creature of the woods, he died in the city; a teller of tales, he found few who would listen; a man of action, he was regarded as passive and helpless. But his fate was not unique: throughout our society, old folks have been segregated into a world of their own. They are no longer the weavers of yarns, the dispensers of wisdom. They are merely decaying, decrepit bodies and are thus pushed aside so that we never have to trouble our minds with the ugly problems they face. And for the old folks of the Edges, the ones who never have accepted the basic assumptions of the space age, the problem is compounded: they are taken involuntarily to urban centers where they are forced, willy-nilly, to live out their time in well-regimented institutions far away from the world they know so well. It must feel, in the final analysis, like being taken prisoner in one's weakest moment, like dying behind enemy lines. Glen, for one, certainly felt that way.

7

Mayme Between Two Worlds

THE INDIAN VILLAGE of Tsurai (now Trinidad) was the first to be discovered by Spanish seamen along the North Coast of California. At the outset the Indians were eager to trade with the newcomers. Showing particular interest in knives and beads, they greeted the anchored boats with their redwood canoes. When their houses were stormed and searched for a deserted sailor, however, the Indians became a bit more wary of their uninvited guests. That was in 1775. By 1817, after several such unfortunate encounters with foreign ships, the Indians of Tsurai had altered their friendly stance. "The Trinidad Indians were ready to receive and massacre us," wrote seaman Peter Correy, "for they are without exception the most savage tribes on all the coast."

The Spanish were followed by the Russians, who hunted down the sea otters in Trinidad Bay. The Russians left once the sea otter population had been depleted, but they were soon followed by the Americans in hot pursuit of gold. Three days after the first permanent white settlers arrived in 1850, an American flag was waving from a sixty-foot pole on top of a hill. The Indians, at best, were simply ignored. The town of Warnersville soon surrounded the Indian village of Tsurai. The deer and elk, so necessary for the Indians' livelihood, began to disappear, and the Indians themselves began to show signs of the white man's illnesses. By 1860, when Indian wars swept across the neighboring countryside, Tsurai had already been transformed from a thriving community into a camp of exiles. The Indians had become strangers in their native land.

The Tsurai "rancheria" survived in its skeletal form until 1916, when logging interests commandeered the spot for a port. The handful of Indians were moved a mile away to a patch of land which had already been stripped of its trees. Today, berry bushes grow out of the charred stumps at the site of Tsurai's second home. The sounds of the freeway can be heard nearby, while the paved roads bear suburban-styled street signs: Ma We Mor View Ln, Pa Pah Ln. Single-story tract houses are flanked by run-down sheds and chicken coops. The driveways are filled with basketball hoops and barking dogs, while the vacant lots are grazed by horses and goats. A single tepee is half erected in one of the yards, although tepees were unknown to the native Indians of California.

Mayme Keparisis, aged seventy, lives alone in her home on the Tsurai rancheria. Her kitchen is electrically equipped, while the living room has wall-to-wall carpeting, acoustical tile on the ceiling, and aluminum-framed windows. Hanging on the plywood veneer walls are dozens of framed family portraits which show Mayme's relatives clad in everything from ceremonial Indian dresses to business suits and white bridal gowns. Also hanging from the walls are an acorn cooking paddle, an eel hook, a winnowing basket—and a picture of Jesus Christ painted on a redwood burl. There are two television sets, one on top of the other. The color set on the bottom has remote control, but it seems to be out of order; the portable set above it is tuned to a fast-shooting Western.

The house belongs to Mayme, but the land it sits on does not. For years Mayme has been engaged in a battle with governmental bureaucracies, trying to get them to grant the Indians separate deeds to their property. "It's just like if I come along and build my house on your property," she says as she sits upright on the sofa, holding her head erect. A stereotyped Indian makes an appearance on the TV Western, but Mayme seems oblivious: she cannot see what's on the tube, for Mayme is almost blind. "You say, 'You're an old woman. You got no place to go. You can build a house on one corner of my ground.' You know, because you felt sorry for me. And when I died, well, the house was yours. That's what the government wants to do with us, but I disagreed."

But Mayme has recently lost interest in her case, for another court case has just been won: the Yurok Indians, of whom Mayme is one, have gained a settlement from the government which will give each individual tens of thousands of dollars as his or her share in the timber-rich Hoopa Indian Reservation nearby. "Lotta people trying to be Indians now that we're getting that money," she says. "But we all have our numbers. We don't have names, we have numbers with our names after them. I forget what my number is. I should tattoo it on my leg."

With money coming in, and Mayme herself advancing in years, the issue concerning the deeds to the land doesn't seem quite so significant any more. "Quit fighting. I get tired of fighting sometimes because all I had to do all my life is fight for what I want. I don't take 'no' for no or 'yes' for yes. And if it's a 'yes' too fast, I want to know the reason why it's too fast. I'm that kind of person. That's how I've got along all my life. And if people say they don't like the looks of me because I'm an Indian, to heck with them. I don't care, because inside of God there's only two people: you're either going to heaven or you're going to hell. That's what the Bible says, so that's all there is to it. And that was my salvation. You either had to be good, or go the other way—away from God."

Yes, Mayme is religious, and she believes in the Christian God. A regular churchgoer, she pays her 10 percent tithe. She was a song leader for years and she speaks proudly of the night she brought the Word of Christ into the hearts of the nonbelieving Indians of Weitchpec. And now that she is about to have money to spare, she knows just what to do with it: "I want to go to the Holy Land when I get that money, to see the ground where Christ walked. I've wanted to do that ever since I learned the white man's way of prayer."

A Christian, perhaps, but Mayme cannot easily forget that she is an Indian as well. "They killed my people all off," she says as an ad for new cars appears on the TV screen. "My grandmother and her one brother and a cousin survived out of the Lake Earl Indians. They marched them up to Gold Beach up in Oregon. And those womens that were pregnant, and old people like me who couldn't walk, they stuck their bayonets in our tummy and just twisted and let our guts drag along. And we fell wherever our guts ended. That's what they did with the Indians, the white people did. That was told to me by my own grandmother that was in that march.

"My grandmother was raised by an old pioneer lady that lived off by herself. But my grandmother's cousin, I guess he was just like old what's-his-name . . . Dillinger. 'Cause he turned to nothing but Hate. He hated, and he killed. He killed with a hatchet. He'd go where the soldiers were sleeping and he'd cut all the ropes around the tent, and when he'd see their head moving, he'd split their head right in two with a hatchet. He killed so many soldiers, and they couldn't catch him. They put a reward on him, and his own people killed him. Killed him for the reward." Do I detect a note of familial or racial pride in her story of a man who would not accept defeat?

Mayme herself was raised by her mother, a full-blooded Yurok. I ask Mayme, "Were the Indians still practicing the old ways when you were young? Were they gathering acorns and things?"

"Yeah, we still do. I do, anyways."

"You gather acorns?"

"Yeah. Even if I have to crawl around on the ground and pick up a rattlesnake, maybe. Course, I didn't last fall because I had too much eye trouble, and they wanted to amputate my leg. I wouldn't let 'em do it. But I had to have eye surgery in the summer. So I didn't pick up acorns last fall. But I take acorns to the school and demonstrate how we grind it and cure it and cook it in my lecture.

"I used to have a picnic on my property every year until I got to be older. I used to have acorns; I have fresh venison; I have salmon fresh, dried, and canned. I have eels fresh and smoked. Then I have seaweed, myrtlenuts, acorns. If I have hazelnuts I put some of that out there, and what-do-you-call-it that we had for breakfast . . . huckleberries. Dried huckleberries. Because that's the way the Indians used to eat. But I had more white people than I had Indians that would come. I had people even coming from L.A. to my picnics."

"How do you prepare the acorns now? Do you leach them in the sand like they used to?"

"No, I use a pan now. Basket pan, I call it. And I put a cloth over it, and use lukewarm water. The first water you put on it comes out like coffee. You keep pouring water on it till it comes out pure, just like it comes out of the faucet.

"And when you make acorn bread, you take your acorn after all the water's run out of it and you press it on your hand just like you do to make hamburger patties, and you put it on a hot rock. You can wrap that up and take it with you for your lunch. You can drink water with that and hunt all day. That's the real Indian bread.

"You know, a man come up one day and said, 'How'd you prepare those acorns?' I said, 'I fixed it in a blender.' He turned to walk away. I said, 'Why should I wear myself out pounding and pounding between my legs? I just put it in a blender and it's all ready to go.' "

"So you've been doing things like cooking acorns and making baskets all your life?"

"No, sir, I haven't. I'm learning with the baskets just like the girls are, to tell you the truth. I can make acorn pots and things, but I never had practice making the baskets. Mother and them were real selfish with their basket materials, so we didn't learn how. We learned all kinds of white men's things—knitting, crocheting, and that kind of stuff."

"So how are you learning to make baskets now? Who are you learning from?"

"I just do it from what I remember seeing my mother do. Just from memory, that's all. I have to think back fifty years. But, you know, it takes a whole year to gather the things that's on a basket. The sticks we pick in the spring. The maidenhair fern we pick next month [June]. The Woodwardia fern we pick in November or December, unless real heavy frost or snow come out; then you can't pick it any more. The bear grass we pick in August. So it takes a whole year to make that little basket if you don't have the material. But just to look at it you go to buy it and you don't think it's worth anything. And all those sticks and things have to be straight. Indians used to say, 'Did you sleep good?' If you slept all squashed up like this, all you're gonna find is crooked roots. But if you slept nice and straight, why then you'll find straight roots that'll split real nice. So if you didn't sleep right, wasn't no use in looking for basket materials that day."

The TV Western is over, and a documentary on snow-mobile racing is now being broadcast into Mayme's living room. But the elderly Indian lady has transported herself back in time, to an era which preceded her own. She begins to speak of the days before the white men came as if she had been there herself.

"You were working all the time, long time ago. You couldn't be lazy a day. You had to go gather your wood for winter. The mens had to go fishing and go get deer meat. And in the fall they had to pick their acorns up and they got their fish in to dry, and if they got the mussels they come and dry the mussels. And they were always doing something *every day*. If you weren't lazy. And if you were lazy, then you would starve to death. Yet they say the Indian is lazy, they say he's dirty. But he took a bath every day, even in the winter. The mens jumped out of the sweathouse right into the river, and the womens bathed in the stream."

Mayme pauses to catch her breath. "You know," she says, "what I'm talking to you about I get twenty-five dollars an hour for. I do. That's what I get paid for it."

"Who pays you twenty-five dollars an hour?"

"You know Uncle Sam?"

"Well, I don't know him personally."

"I do. Because he pays me my Social Security also."

"So you're on a pretty intimate basis with him?"

"And the government puts so much money away for Indian culture."

"Who do you tell it all to during that hour? Is it for kids, or professional anthropologists, or . . . ?"

"It's for *everybody*. I go into churches, I go into ladies' clubs, and I go to the university and I go to high schools and grammar schools. Now the young folks, they're out lecturing too, but what do they know? They don't know nothing but what they read, only what somebody told somebody else years and years ago that didn't have no interpreter. They study that and go tell that, but they're all wrong. We're trying to correct the wrong that they made, and it's kinda hard sometimes. I been through several different professors. They come right here to my house."

"They come right here?"

"Yes, sir. I teach classes right in this very room. I've been in this work for twenty-five years. People ask me, 'Why don't you use any papers?' I never read from papers when I teach. Didn't when I used to preach either. We Indians had to have our papers right up here." She points to her head with one hand, and grasps her white cane with the other. "If I been an old grandma telling a story, I have three people right in front of me and I have them repeat it after me so they get it just right."

Mayme, in short, has become a professional Indian. In these times of increasing interest in the Indian way of life, she and others like her have finally found eager ears for their stories and inherited wisdom. This cultural resurgence, furthermore, has created new markets for Mayme's Indian artifacts: baskets, beads, weapons, etc. Mayme was once offered $1,000 for an arrow that was used in the Indian wars, while she herself paid out $1,200 for a string of original trade beads from the old Hudson's Bay Company. (How strange that a symbol of the first contact with white civilization is valued so highly by the Indians!) The Yuroks as a people have always been interested in the acquisition of personal wealth, and now, as always, they wear their beads proudly for public occasions. Prices being what they are, however, it has become increasingly dangerous to be too loose with one's treasures, and Mayme, along with some of her friends, now keeps her most valuable Indian treasures in the safe-deposit box in the bank.

It is difficult to determine whether this acquisitive interest in historical possessions is due to Yurok or Anglo culture, to the increased interest in Indian heritage or to a more mundane participation in the middle-class game of outdoing the Joneses. Indeed, it is difficult to determine just which cultural milieu Mayme belongs in. She has balanced herself on the seemingly precarious Edge between the Indian and the Christian universe, between traditional artifacts and modern, new-fangled conveniences. Apparently oblivious to the fact that it was the Western and Christian way of life that did in the Indians, she sees no inherent contradiction in remaining on the interface which separates opposing peoples and cultures. But then again, why should she? She has managed to cope with the world as it was presented to her: she was born an Indian in twentieth-century America. Logically, the cultures might appear in conflict, but that is not to deny the possibility of a successful personal integration within the context of apparent social contradictions. Mayme stands as a tribute to the strength of the human spirit through adaptability. On an analytical or political level, the Edges might be fraught with tension, but a flexible individual can at least minimize the human toll.

The basic unit of Yurok society has always been the family. Blood ties were paramount in determining friends and enemies, and who owed what to whom. Today, nearly everybody in the Tsurai rancheria seems to be related to each other: Mayme's sister lives across the street, her daughter is in the trailer up the way, while her cousins are next door and down the block. "Well," says Mayme by way of explanation, "my great-grandfather had twelve wives, so you get a lot of relatives that way."

Yet there aren't many full-blooded Indians left on the rancheria. "The Indians all married white men, or else they married white women," Mayme says regretfully. But Mayme herself has been married twice—both times to white men. Her three children, therefore, are only half Indian, and they have showed little interest in the Indian culture that Mayme still feels a part of herself. "I'm sorry," she says, "but I wish I could keep them in my own ways. But it's hard."

"Why didn't you ever marry an Indian?" I ask her.

"The mens drink too much, and what don't drink smokes marijuana. That's why I didn't marry one. They didn't have marijuana them days, but they drank too much. And I wouldn't have a drunkard. I didn't want to be married to a drunkard 'cause my dad was killed when he was drunk. Train ran over him when I was two years old. I didn't know him, and I was raised without a father. I've had to work since I was thirteen years old. And I'm still taking care of myself. If I can find a man that'll buy all my clothes and all my groceries to eat and everything in the house, I'll be his slave. And I'll say, 'Yes, dear. Yes, dear.' You know, jump up and wait on him hand and foot. But I haven't found him yet, and I don't think I ever will. Now, till that day comes, I'll be my own boss."

When Mayme was eighteen years old, her family wanted to sell her to the neighbor next door. Sell her? Yes, for according to Indian law that's how marriages were arranged. The family of the groom would have to pay the family of the bride to compensate for the loss of her services, with an additional payment to be made upon the birth of each child. Well into the twentieth century, the Yuroks dutifully made and accepted payments for marriages and births. I ask Mayme: "Do people still believe in the Indian laws today?"

"The old people, yes. They say, 'What's that paper you get married with? You can make a fire with it, you can use it out in the rest room.' A marriage license isn't worth nothing to an Indian, because they used to give two hundred fifty, three hundred dollars for a wife, and sometimes maybe more. They look at your hands. If your hands is just like silk, they won't buy you, 'cause you're lazy, you don't do nothing. You find a girl that's got hands like mine—rough, look like they work hard— then that's the one they buy, 'cause she's not lazy."

"How about the younger folks today? Which marriage laws do they follow?"

"Well, far as I look, they don't follow any laws, white men laws or Indian laws. And the whites are doing the same, aren't they? So you don't follow God's laws either, 'cause God's laws say you have to be married. If you get a girl in trouble, you haven't committed a sin if you marry her."

"When you talk about 'God's laws,' which God do you mean? White men's God or the Indian God?"

"How many Gods is there? The Indian has the same God as you've got, if you're a Christian. They say that we came from the earth, that the earth is our mother. Because God created man from dust, didn't He? That's what the Bible says, if you know your Bible. And then He took a rib out of this man and made a woman. And the Indian say that when we die we go back to our Mother Earth. And when they get to heaven, they don't have to be servants. That's the Indian law. They can sit around enjoy singing and seeing people dance—jump dance, brush dance, and everything like that. But if you are stingy and don't have nothing, you have to be a slave up there. You have to work for those other people. That's what the Indian believe in: that there is a God up in heaven that's watching everything you do. And what the Indian believe, close as I can say, is just like the Old Testament.

"But like I say, once you're an Indian, you're just *born* an Indian. I lost two babies, one right after the other. I was crying, I was all in tears when I lost my baby boy. I was down on the ground picking up acorns. (I picked up nine sacks of acorns that year. That's a lot of acorns, because they tell us to pick up a lot when there's a lot, because you don't know how many years there might not be any.) So I was crying and crying, and once a breeze came up on the hill, and a song came to me. It was just like somebody was singing it to me. So I learned it. And when my mother came up afterwards, I said, 'Mom, I learned an Indian song when I was picking up acorns.' She says, 'You sing it to me. I'll tell you what it is.' So I sing it for her. She almost fainted. She says, 'Mayme, who ever taught you that song?' I said, 'The wind did.' She says, 'You heard that someplace.' I says, 'No, no place in my life.' She says it was my great-grandfather—that was his war dance." Mayme pauses for a moment, closes her eyes, and proceeds to sing her song movingly: single syllables, almost like a chant, with a yell at the end. Then she explains: "He says in his words, 'Enemies, you locked me up.' But he got out. He was on top of the hill when he sang it. He says, 'Come and get me now. I'm your enemy. And I'm out!' They never did get him.

"Now, where in the world did that song come from? Tell me, 'cause it's a mystery to me. Since you folks is so educated, tell me. Why would that song come to me? Once an Indian, always an Indian. There's a spirit—is it flying through the air, or what is it? You're talking to me here now, it goes into the timbers and into everything here, and a hundred years from now somebody's going to breathe that same air and hear the things that we're talking about now. Is it possible?

"And when I was down on the beach having my picture taken for the professors, I was picking the mussels, and I cried. I said, 'God, oh God, how many people has picked mussels here? Now I'm picking mussels here to show in the movies how we used to live, so they'll know how *hard* we used to work for our food. The white people can see it and our children can see it, and our Indian people who don't know much about being Indians can see it. Let me do what's right and say what's right.' And the most beautiful song came to me. The most beautiful song I ever heard, but it hasn't come to me again. Now where did that song come from? It's a mystery to me yet."

8

The Last Great Days
of the Vance Hotel

THE FOGHORN NEVER STOPS in Humboldt Bay because the fog is always there. The gray mist envelops the Eureka waterfront, with its sporadic warehouses and fisheries, scrap-metal yards and vacant lots dotted with poison hemlock. Sandwiched between First Street, which is the waterfront, and Fourth Street, which is Highway 101, lies a thin stretch of land which, years ago, was the main part of town. Today, half the storefronts are deserted, the paint peeling from their lavish Victorian façades. Those that are still in use are junk and repair shops, card rooms and bars, and cheap hotels. The people who remain are mostly old, poor, and/or drunk; looking down upon them from a giant billboard is a picture of Mark Spitz, young and beautiful, drinking a glass of milk.

Eureka is the only town on the North Coast of California big enough for a skid row. It is here that old loggers, fishermen, and railroaders, with neither home nor family, have come to live out their time. But it is a skid row with a home-town touch, for the place is still small enough for the people to know their neighbors. They may be drunk—but you won't get lost or mugged on Third and F or Second and D. It's the safest skid row around.

On the corner of Second and G, the words "Vance Hotel" are neatly inscribed in the sidewalk; above, the four tall stories of the 101-year-old Vance fade into the fog. A sign in front reads "Western Music—Dancing Nightly," but the Vance Log Cabin is all boarded up, as is the Vance Cafe. Only the hotel itself remains open, with sixty of its one hundred rooms taken by elderly men and women on a fairly permanent basis. Twenty of the rooms have been eliminated from use, while the remainder are let out to transients for three, four, or five dollars a night.

Through the arched entrance is a spacious lobby with a tile floor, wooden paneling on the walls, and a majestic staircase leading up to the rooms. The wood and tile are holding up well, but that is not enough: the sofas and chairs are falling apart at the seams, the neon sign saying "Gents" is tilted downward, and two of the three telephone stalls have had their phones taken away. Doors that look like they once led to somewhere important now lead to nowhere, and a row of vending machines gives the place the feel of a bus terminal. It was not always thus at the Vance. There were once meals in the banquet room, and waiters and bellhops to service the well-to-do travelers. Room 210, the Honeymoon Suite, was elaborately furnished with an expensive red carpet and a round bed with a red velvet bedspread.

Today, the single elderly gentleman who lives behind the ten-foot door to Room 210 goes out every night to play cards. The corridor outside his room is dimly lit by a single electric light bulb, its wires hanging precariously from bent-over nails fifteen feet above the worn-through carpet underfoot. Other doors, smaller than his, stretch a line on either side of the hallway. The rooms within are painted a dull green and pink, with a white patch on the wall around the sink to give the air of a bathroom. Fancy curlicues deck the steam radiators, which are never on. Faded shades and curtains made of a gauze-like non-material cover the windows, which either won't open at all or, if they do, won't stay that way. The beds are overly soft. There is always a chest of drawers, but that is all: even the Gideon Bibles are lacking.

The walls are paper-thin. A voice on the other side speaks to a pet bird: ". . . lover . . . baby . . ."

Fred and Misha, neighboring singles, keep track of each other by the sounds they make.

"I didn't hear you come in last night," Misha says in the lobby.

"I never went out," says Fred, a retired brakeman. "Slept right through."

"Fred, you got some cigarettes here?"

"What do you want, cigarettes?"

"Yeah."

"I'll get you one." He pulls out a Camel.

"No, wait—I don't want one of these son of a . . ."

"Well, these are good cigarettes. You don't know the difference anyway."

"What's the name of them?"

"Pall Mall. That's the kind you smoke, isn't it?"

"I want you to get me a pack."

"A pack will make you sick. You're too young to smoke anyway."

"I didn't have enough to eat today," she says.

"That's the reason you shouldn't smoke today. You're gonna starve to death, you know that."

"I think I will," she admits.

"You eat all them oranges and bananas I got you?"

"No, I ate the bananas. I still got one."

"What about them oranges? You eat any of them?"

"I ate one."

"Well, I got you six. You drink that milk?"

"Yeah."

"You're gonna get you a bellyache, then."

Misha and Fred are regulars at the Vance. "I been here two or three different times," she says. "I go away and then I come back. I always stop here when I come to town. I have nowhere else to go. It just seems like home to me. I had a husband that died here. It makes me feel, well, like I just belong here."

Over on the couch, Luther, whose back is giving him trouble, is downing a hot dinner which somebody has brought back from Peggy's, the cafe down the block. Kenny, the desk clerk, brings him some coffee from the vending machine. For Kenny and those who will spell him later on, the Vance is more than just a job—it's a way of life. Their lives are integrally linked with those of their clientele. Many of the clerks live in the hotel, calling each other up on the house phone to see what's happening downstairs. They run a sort of barstool confessional at one end of the main desk, engaging the old-timers in casual conversation. "Another service," says Eunice, who often works swing shift, "is we play cards with anybody who wants to. We have about five hundred sets of cards. I specialize in rummy and Kenny specializes in double solitaire and Karen [the manager] specializes in cribbage.

"Everybody here looks after each other," Eunice continues. She'll turn the light on inside the room for the elderly woman who's afraid of the dark; she'll offer her friendship to those grieved by the loss of a friend or relative. In return, Eunice receives token mementos of appreciation: an elderly woman just gave her a string of bells which had been a present from her deceased husband nineteen years ago. "Sometimes I think I should get out of skid row and do something with myself," says Eunice. "But I'm just too involved with the people."

Years back, there was a bellhop named Glen Jarmin who slowly worked his way up the hotel ladder. Finally, it is rumored, he won the Vance in a poker game. Now a tire salesman who lives out of town, Jarmin has a policy of not raising rents on the old-timers who have been there for years.

But rumor also has it that ownership of the Vance is about to change hands. Plans have already been approved by the Redevelopment Agency for a thorough renovation which will turn the run-down rooms into small efficiency apartments. I ask Bill, who used to work in the woods, if he knows anything about the plans.

"Naw, I heard there's supposed to be a tourist outfit come through here. Rebuild the whole town, you know."

"From what I hear," I tell him, "they're going to put apartments in here. Do you think they'll raise the rents?"

"I imagine they will. I don't know what the hell they're gonna do. I'm gonna buy me a tent and move out into the country," he adds jokingly.

I mention to Alfred, a retired lumberman, that they're intending to fix the place up.

"Oh, they are?" he asks, seemingly surprised.

"Do you know anything about that?"

"No, I haven't heard anything about it."

I ask Duke Wilson if he knows what they plan to do.

"No idea. I heard they was gonna make apartments out of it and build a dining room back here and . . . You never know what they plan to do. Too many stories."

Outside the picture window in the lobby of the Vance, the false front of an old Victorian mansion rises abruptly from a pile of rubble in the lot behind it. The fancy two-dimensional façade, spared by the bulldozers that have been pounding mercilessly away at the rest of the building, gives the distinct appearance of a Hollywood movie set. A new structure will soon emerge in place of the old, but, thanks to the efforts of the historically conscious Eureka Redevelopment Agency, the original front has been preserved.

Inside the Vance, the TV is tuned to the late-evening news. Someone tries to change the channel, but to no avail: there's nothing on but more news. The image on the screen is of a hearing room full of businessmen and professional people; the sound track reveals that the subject under discussion is Eureka's "Olde Towne" project. The Redevelopment Agency is giving its progress report: 20 percent of the funds have already been spent, and contracts will soon be announced for putting cobblestone sidewalks and mini-parks along Second Street, just down the block from the Vance.

But no one's listening to the voice on the tube, for a drunken resident has just staggered in. Considerable attention is given to how the man can best be enticed to his room or, failing that, how he can be forcibly removed. After the desk clerk finally maneuvers the drunk into the doorless elevator, several blank stares are redirected toward the TV screen. This time a pair of well-dressed women are politely discussing the activities of the

Eureka Heritage Association, but, once again, no one cares to listen. The discussion might well affect the Vance and the neighborhood around it, yet all the residents can see are two fancy ladies talking about some nonsense or other. Only when *Torpedo Run* appears on the Late Show does serious television watching begin.

With all the interest—and all the money—directed toward the Olde Towne area, the place is sure to change. In many ways the changes will be welcomed by the residents: nobody particularly likes living on a skid row, even though Eureka's is as good as they come. I ask Duke Wilson if he enjoys living where he does. "No," he says flatly. "The elevator's out of order two or three times a week. I don't even get in the thing, I walk up. Or the furniture—they won't even spend a dime on it. Look at that thing you're sitting on: it's a disgrace."

"What would you do with the Vance if you owned it?"

"Well, I don't know. In the first place, I wouldn't own it. If I had money enough to buy it, I sure wouldn't buy it. It's in the wrong part of town. This part of town is shot."

"But what about the redevelopment project?"

"All this renovating out in the street here is a waste of the taxpayer's money. Absolutely. Not in this part of town. Who's gonna come down here? The businessmen won't come down here any more. You think for a minute one of them would come down here and rent a room? No, sir. And those fountains they're putting in—all there'll be in those places is winos, sitting around drinking wine."

But the redevelopment folks think otherwise. All those plazas, trees, and ornamental hitching posts are not intended for the drunks. Because of the physical improvements, they expect the character of the neighborhood to be uplifted. Gift shops and boutiques, it is hoped, will replace the card rooms and bars, while tourists will replace the bums. I ask an official at the Redevelopment Agency: "What do you think will happen to the older residents of the area?"

"We're not going to run them out," he says, "but the economics will make them gradually fade." Where, I ask, will they fade *to?* "I don't know," he admits. "Maybe to Oakland or San Francisco. There's nowhere up here where I can see them going."

To Oakland or San Francisco! So even the skid rows are becoming centralized in the major metropolitan areas. The time used to be when nearly every stop on the railroad was a place for the down-and-out, while every lumber town throughout the countryside had its "skid row" built up beside the "skid roads" that led to the mills (indeed, this is how the term was derived). The folks who make the Vance their home might not love it here, but they'd rather be here than elsewhere. Even Duke, embittered as he is, admits to a certain feeling for the place: "I like the area, like the climate. And I like the fish—lotta good fishing around here."

What *will* happen to these former woodsmen and fishermen once the redevelopment of Olde Towne has made them "fade"? And what will happen to the many older women who can easily survive at the Vance but for whom the big cities mean only danger and fear? If not to the cities, they might drift toward the suburban-style rest homes on the outskirts of town. There, they will be isolated from the world, outcasts in space as well as time. No more bars, no shops nearby, no freedom to do as they please —they will pass the rest of their days in a world that is not their own.

For all its run-down appearance, the Vance has something of great importance to offer to the elderly singles set. The residents can stay involved with everyday life: they can shop down the street, or go out on the town at night. They visit each other in their rooms, come together in the lobby, and even go out on dates. They strike up conversations and sometimes relationships with young transients who share their hotel, and with the young clerks who understand their needs. And, in their way, they get to take care of each other.

"Seems like you're trying to kill yourself," says one old-timer to another, who appears to have been drinking too much.

"Seems that way," replies the drunk.

"Why run away from it?" says the friend. "You've got to take life the way it is. This world don't owe you nothing, so don't expect nothing. Then you won't get so upset. Take what you can get and don't run away." Here at the Vance, you can counsel as well as be counseled; you can help control the problem of drunks, even if that might mean yourself.

A little renovation is long overdue in and around the Vance. Yet how strange it is that in the name of historical restoration, the real history—the history that is still going on—is forgotten. They save the false fronts to the buildings, but who is saving the old-timers who will soon be displaced? Where will the old folks of the Edges go when they're feeling down and out? Indeed, where can they *afford* to go? To urban slums, to suburban institutions—farther and farther away from anyplace they might call home. Eureka's Olde Towne, their small-town city, will be priced beyond their reach.

Part Four
YOUNG FOLKS

We have brought with us the notion that we want to start all over and develop for ourselves a new lifestyle combining the primitive pioneer spirit of our forefathers, the most modern and most ancient of architectural modes, tools, and technology, and above all a new awareness, or consciousness, if you will, of the world we are a part of and our relationship to it. . . .

We also wished to retire from the watchful eye of the government. Why? Not because we intended illegal or illicit activities, but because we have begun to express a traditional conservative belief that a man's home is his private domain.

—FROM A PAMPHLET DISTRIBUTED BY UNITED STAND, AN ORGANIZATION OF NEW PIONEERS

9
Scraping By

THE MEDIAN FAMILY INCOME in the United States is over $12,000 per year. Throughout the backhills of northern California, however, there are young families who live on a mere fraction of that amount—and who don't seem to mind it at all. They drive secondhand cars, wear secondhand clothes, and, most significantly, are building up their homesteads on secondhand land— land which has been overlogged and overgrazed, land which had been deemed agriculturally worthless until the young folks came along with their chickens and goats and organically fertilized gardens.

Most of these rural émigrés were born and raised within the context of the twentieth-century Metropolis. Why did they leave it? What did they hope to gain by abandoning their telephones and televisions, by reversing the trend toward an ever more complex technology? Why have they voluntarily opted for rural poverty rather than urban wealth?

Partly, they sought out the countryside as a means of escape, an opportunity to live with the trees and flowers, clean air and clean water, and a little peace and quiet near their homes. But they also wanted something else: to gain a measure of control over the physical dynamics of their personal lives. Food, shelter, clothing, water, and energy—the basic realities of what it takes to maintain human life on earth—were theirs for the asking, but the genesis of how these necessities were satisfied lay well concealed beneath the complexities of mass production and corporate structures. Food came from the store, not from the farm; electricity came in the form of a monthly bill. Even in the worst of weather, it was easy to stay warm and dry. Life in the Metropolis, in short, had come to be taken for granted.

To rediscover what it was all about, the self-styled new pioneers decided to start from scratch: to grow their own food, build their own houses, generate their own heat and energy. Singly, in families, in communes—people in their twenties and thirties have literally flocked to the American countryside in recent years, creating a mass migration which has taken on the significance of a bona fide social movement. Abandoned homesteads have been suddenly restored, forgotten towns suddenly remembered. And the old-time ranchers and loggers who once thought they had been bypassed by modern civilization now find themselves very much in demand as the newcomers seek out the practical know-how which they never learned in school. "We're all ears," says a young woman named Anon. "We want to know everything people can tell us about raising crops and livestock. You ask one of the old-time farmers about something like that and you open a Pandora's box—you better be ready to stay all day."

Homesteading in the late twentieth century, however, is an altogether different matter from what it was fifty or a hundred years ago. Roads and automotive transportation make the back-hills more accessible now than they have ever been before. Modern inventions such as plastic water pipe and transparent, weatherproof vinyl enable a homestead to spring up almost overnight. A wealth of surplus and salvaged goods from the overabundant American economy furnish the homesteaders with instant clothing and building materials. And for those who cannot do it all by themselves, a variety of welfare programs are ready, albeit not very willing, to help them out.

Although they seek knowledge and inspiration from the past, the new homesteaders are more than willing to adapt the technology of the present and the future to suit their own needs. They experiment with windmills, water generators, and solar ovens. They would like to convert their own personal waste into fertilizer for their gardens and methane gas with which they might someday run their cars. They have perfected the geodesic dome, a lightweight architectural innovation which serves them well, off in the woods. Even the manner in which they grow and gather their food is constantly being adjusted as they learn from each other's experiments—and mistakes. A new-styled woodsman named Mark, for instance, is going to try to raise hogs on acorns and grubs by building a wooden fence around his second-growth forest. "But that's just another one of my bizarre experiments," he admits. "I've gone through so many of them. Everyone does it. Everyone puts in their own little experiments, and then everyone else learns from that. How to grow vegetables out of solid rock, or how to make houses out of bark. You do what you can."

From the standpoint of the long-time local residents, the spectacle which is unfolding in their own back yards appears rather strange indeed. Just where, they ask, did these people all come from? And why, of all places, did they decide to come *here?* How do they expect to make a living off of bankrupt land? "I can't figure out how these people can make a living off sixty acres of that stuff," says Johnnie Chambers, a well-established rancher. "Our forefathers couldn't do it—they starved out. Eventually that land will all revert back, possibly, unless some kind of industry comes in here. That would bring in some work and some money into the country, and these people on these sixty acres then could go out and get a job and survive. But to live off sixty acres, to make a living off it, there's just no way in the world. You might run a cow or two, or a goat or two, or even half a dozen cows, but you can't survive on that."

Yet somehow they *are* managing to survive. Not all of them, for sure—some still depend on welfare or money from elsewhere, while others have not taken well to country ways and have already returned to the cities whence they came. But many of the folks have indeed managed to adapt to the land, to discover a means of a livelihood in their new environment. By living simply, raising some (although seldom all) of their food, providing their own shelter, heating and cooking with energy that lies rotting in the woods, and generally servicing their own needs from their own resources whenever and wherever they can, they have managed to subsist on very little hard, cold cash.

Still, they do need a little—perhaps a thousand dollars a year per person, or maybe two thousand if they can manage that much. Unlike their nineteenth-century mentors, the new homesteaders can rarely approach total self-sufficiency on the land. Many of the natural resources that were available a century ago are lacking today, while the needs and desires of these modern-day souls are often more demanding than those of their predecessors. In one way or another, they must find a way to make some money now and then. How do they scrape it together out there in the woods? They fish, they farm, they engage in crafts for sale—whatever they find that works. For each person or family the formula is different.

MICHAEL AND JUDY, FARMERS

Michael: When we came to this area, I think we had maybe a hundred dollars—but also a truck and a chain saw and wedges. From that, we were able to survive working in the woods, but it certainly wasn't building up much money. And then I went to work for Bob [McKee, a local land dealer] with the idea that I'd be working off the payments for our land.

Ray: But how did you get the money for the rest of it—the livestock, the house . . . ?

Judy: Bits and pieces. Everything came a little bit this way and a little bit that way. The government helped with the fencing. We were able to get some money ahead for that.

Michael: The posts I make, but we have to buy the fencing. And the staples too. I can appreciate a government program like that. It says: You can make the posts and do the labor, and we'll provide the thing that you have to put the cash outlay for. But the beauty of fencing that very few people recognize is that you end up spending a certain length of time in a particular spot that you wouldn't ordinarily spend some time being at. You see the world from that spot, and then you move onto another spot that's close, very similar, but just a little bit different. And you do this through the whole fencing project.

Judy: It's a beautiful progression. The soils are different, the terrain . . .

Michael: Every time you take a shovelful of dirt out, you're seeing something that you've never seen before. It's exciting.

Ray: How about this house? That must have run into some money.

Michael: Five hundred dollars. That's for the main part, which is sixteen by twenty-eight feet. But the new part didn't cost much more, 'cause it was all milled right here. You've got to scrounge. Like Dimmick's mill went out of business, and he had one-by-tens there for sixty-five bucks a thousand. That was the siding, planking, and everything. The poles we got from the land. And the barn—that didn't cost us anything. I split all my own shakes.

Ray: What kind of farm do you see yourselves as running? Do you plan to specialize in a particular animal or crop?

Michael: Our land here is what a well-rounded farm would look like if you reduced the scale maybe four or five times. Walk out to the orchard and you see just twenty, thirty trees. If you were to have a real orchard, you'd have five acres of them. We have it all condensed to one acre.

Judy: We do have plans for using another part of our land for a walnut and chestnut orchard. I'm nurturing the trees now. We envision that kind of diversification as ultimately being our way of making it. We can develop a few acres of nut orchards, and if they're well tended . . .

Michael: That's our old-age pension. We need all the other stuff in the meantime.

Ray: How much land do you have, and how much stock do you have on it?

Michael: We have about a hundred and sixty acres. We're only using about half of it now. Right now we have two milk cows and three steers and four nanny goats and half a dozen sheep. People buy milk from us. Just lately we've been living entirely on that.

Ray: How much milk do you get?

Michael: Well, this year I found a way of keeping production up by cutting my own hay and also making silage from corn. We cut the corn, put it through the shredder, then bagged it in plastic bags, making them airtight. Of course, now I'm thinking about plans for a silo 'cause it seems to work so well. It keeps your production up. Right now she's not fresh, but she's still giving me four gallons a day.

Ray: Only one cow is milking?

Michael: The other is giving, but I'm letting her calf nurse. But this four gallons we get, somehow we end up selling only two gallons a day. We sell it for a buck fifty a gallon.

Ray: And that's your whole income—three dollars a day?

Michael: Well, there's no one thing that you can say: This is how we make it. We just live with what we got. Like we consider that we raise a steer for two years to pay our taxes. That's the way it seems to run. But this year we traded our steer to Stan Randall for work with the Cat—he built our reservoirs and some roads so I could bring my tractor out to the fields. So everything's fluid, everything's moving around. You can't pin it down and say: We make it from here. Now we're making money from milk; soon we'll be selling garlic.

Judy: We decided we were going to raise garlic this year as our first venture into a cash crop because it would be most foolproof. Garlic isn't temperamental as to soil or weather requirements, and you don't have to harvest it instantly or sell it instantly. So with very high hopes, we planted a half acre. Well, after breaking up all those cloves and planting them and watering them all summer by hand, it was time to let the crop dry out. It was mature. As we did that, the grasshoppers moved in and began to devastate the area. They began to eat what we thought would never be eaten. *Nobody* was supposed to eat garlic. It was supposed to be deer-proof and insect-proof. So we brought in the chickens to eat the grasshoppers, which worked fairly well. It's really been a wonderful learning process. Now we know that there is no such thing as an easy crop—every crop has its particular quirks, its own peculiarities. If you're aware of them, you know how to work around them. But when you're new at something, everything is a monumental problem.

Ray: What do you have in the way of poultry?

Michael: We started out with half a dozen hens. But chickens tend to spread. We don't even count them now. Geese, too. You start out with a couple and you end up with more. But we can never get more ducks. The raccoons seem to know exactly when the eggs will hatch, and the whole works disappears.

Judy: I'd say we have about two dozen laying hens now.

Michael: We sell eggs. When we have a surplus of *anything* we unload it—give it away, trade it, or sell it. If you go into town, you bring whatever surplus you have. Some days we can chalk up a plus sign going into town and buying things, 'cause we can actually bring more into town than what we take out. That's not how you "make it," but that's sort of how you can keep going.

Ray: What do you do with your sheep?

Judy: I raise the sheep primarily for the wool. I use it myself, and I sell it to people who are interested in spinning. But we have lost sheep every year to dogs. This year we lost a purebred ram. He was a lovely creature with great curved horns and long, curly silver and black wool. But he is no more. Our sheep are like pets, we have such a small flock. When we see them dead or dying, it's a very hard loss to take. Dogs are the one thing we can't control.

Michael: The only thing I can do is every time I hear a dog bark and I know it's chasing, I go and try to kill it. It's the only way you can survive with sheep.

Ray: Are you to the point where you produce most of your own food yourselves?

Judy: Oh, absolutely. Except for grains. We don't produce rice, millet, oatmeal. Or salt. But we would like to produce wheat.

Michael: It's hard to grow your own grain, 'cause then you have to have equipment to thrash it. But we do produce corn, cornmeal. If we had to get down to a corn-grain diet, we could do it. It's just that we're able to afford the diversity now.

Ray: Just grains alone wouldn't seem to run into much of a grocery bill, if you're not using it for your animals too.

Michael: But if it's the only thing you buy, you see it. When we go into Evergreen, that's what we buy.

Judy: I can a lot, and then we have winter squashes, pumpkins, and some potatoes. We keep a winter garden going as best we can—beets and carrots, chard and cabbage.

Michael: And meat—we have all the beef we can use.

Ray: How do you preserve it?

Michael: We have a freezer down in town.

Ray: With all these animals to care for, do you ever get to take any vacations?

Judy: We can if we get a baby-sitter for this place. Last year during the winter we took our first trip away in three years. It was in February, the time of the big storm. So the poor people that baby-sat this place had every problem imaginable thrown at them. The water went out, it was drenching rain the whole time, they had no experience milking cows. And the highway was closed off, so we couldn't get home. We were so worried, it wasn't much of a vacation.

Ray: How long were you gone?

Michael: Four days.

Ray: And that was your only vacation in three years?

Michael: Yeah. We're kind of attached to the place. I can find more fulfillment being here, doing what I'm doing, than I can find anywhere else.

Judy: It's our big project, this place. It's all engrossing at this point.

Michael: And the animals—you might see them as our "village." The milk cows, the calves, the goats, and the sheep are all villagers.

Judy: And the geese all have their personalities. We raised one gosling here—we hatched it out in a basket on top of the stove, with a hot-water bottle, wrapped in fleece. And that goose, though fully grown, is still our gosling. There's all those little things. . . .

Michael: I think we get the same stimulation and diversity as most people get, being outside all the time. It's so rewarding, it's continually growing on you. And growth is always unexpected—it has its own way. When something grows, it's its own self. So it's ever-changing, whether it's a kid that's growing, or a tree, or grass. Every year you see something new happening. Or sometimes it's always been happening and you just happened to notice it, so *you've* grown.

KEITH, A METALWORKER

The basic way I make my living is at my shop doing ironwork and metal repair. It goes all the way from doing handmade stuff for people in the city who want real nice things and don't care how much it costs to fixing people's broken necessities, like their stoves. But a lot of the reason for why I make my living that way is the tools. They're my toys. That doesn't mean that I don't use them for legitimate, real things, but the only way you can justify having all those tools is to use them to make money with, too. A lot of the work I do for other people just supports my habit.

My father was never into tools or anything like that, but when I was in the fifth grade I started hanging around Bill's Flying A down on the corner. I never learned anything official about metalwork there, but I did come in contact with the tools. Even before that, I always used to lay under the coffee table and pretend I was working on it. I used to like to take things apart, too. They were usually watches and clocks, so I couldn't get them back together.

Then when I first started thinking about moving to the country, I thought I'd like to—I thought I'd *have* to—have metalworking tools. So I took a class. Then I took another class, and this far-out teacher I had was into "realistic education." He taught what you wanted to learn. I was building the back onto my school bus at that time, so I could carry livestock around. I thought I could just squat here and there and have this livestock with me on the bus. But he said: instead of putting some goats back there, why don't you put a set of torches on it and then you could always make some money with it? So I did, and started doing it on the streets of Berkeley. I didn't do that for long—maybe two weeks—before I was ready to leave the city. I came up here and started to work on Peter's boat the day after I got here.

That was how I started here. I started working off the back
of my bus. At that point hardly anybody around here had any
money to pay for anything, so it was maybe just five bucks here
and there. I remember my first big job was when Yerba hired me
to make racks on her car for eighteen bucks. I was really im-
pressed that she hired me, really flattered. *Eighteen dollars!* So I
did it. I mean, I had been working for other people for a long
time, but nobody was willing to pay for it. But you'd be surprised how much more money there is around here now than
there was three years ago. Three years ago nobody was working, or had anything going. Now a lot of different people have
something going to bring in a few bucks. So now people pay, or
at least enough of them do.

Things go in runs. All of a sudden three various parties need
pickup racks, so you start thinking, gee, maybe there's a big
market in pickup racks. Then all of a sudden someone starts
wanting something else, like an elaborate steel gate that ranchers
have with a sliding thing over the padlock so people can't shoot
it off. And every fall, or not until almost winter, there's a big
run on stoves. Last year I was manufacturing those barrel stoves.
I bought the cast-iron parts from the manufacturer and picked
up the drums from Burrill's [a local junkyard] or from anywhere, just so long as they hadn't had any gasoline in them, since
they might explode when you work on it. A barrel stove is the
cheapest large stove you can get. For seventy-five dollars, you
can get a stove that'll heat a real large area.

But when I first came here, I definitely wasn't making my
total living off ironwork. I did a lot of buying and selling. I'd
find stoves that needed repair, get 'em cheap and fix 'em up and
sell 'em. Or cars, too. At that time, and probably still at this
time, if you want to make your living around here you have to
be as versatile as possible and be ready to do whatever comes
your way.

Of course, back then you could get a lot of your stuff from
the dump. The Whitethorn dump, every time you'd go there
you'd find something good. I don't know why, but they took
the old Whitethorn dump and filled it in and closed it up and
tried to sell it as a piece of land. They put this dumpster in by

the junction instead. Somehow, when they did that the quality of the garbage, the trash, went way down. For some reason, people just weren't throwing away the same quality stuff they were throwing away before. It just didn't make sense. But then again, over the years I've realized that a lot of the stuff I used to take wasn't worth taking. I've changed my outlook on what is valuable and what isn't. I'm more selective, I know more what I want.

The thing about going to the dump, though, is it's always fun, so it's never a waste of time. When I lived in Colorado, the dumps there were all covered by state law. One thing that's outlawed there is scrounging—by anybody. It's kind of ridiculous. So what we used to do is after hours we'd backpack into the dump cross-country, from a different direction from where the guy would drive out. That was really fun. I don't know if it was worth it as far as what we got, but it sure was fun. Although one time we went real late, and all the skunks that lived in all the wrecked cars were out, and we walked right into the middle of them.

Then we used to live next to the New Mexico border, so we used to drive down into New Mexico, where it was legal, and pick at the dump. Once there was an old Indian woman and her young son scrounging, and they were on horseback and they had saddlebags where they put their stuff.

We still stop at dumps now and then. We still stop at Safeway garbage, too. The pickings are a little scarce there now, but we got a fifty-pound sack of dog food that had been torn open, and we got a case of green olives and a case of pickles—somebody had dropped them and broke one jar, and they threw the whole thing away. So it's worth it sometimes. You've got to scrounge to get by out here.

MARK, A WOODSMAN

To start with, I wanted to get away from any civilization trips, towns and all the amenities that went with it. Just so I could understand where it all was coming from. So I got a piece of land that had no road, since I figured roads were the main link of communication between civilization and just the raw woods. But then, not having a road, I had no way of really building any kind of house in there, except to depend on natural materials. In this area that was easy because of all the redwood trees—the logging of the redwood trees left a lot of salvage on the ground. So I found out from the old guys around how to make split stuff with the wedges, the hammers, the prying bars. There was just enough junk lying up there on the ground, like bark and big chunks of logs and pieces that were already split off, so that I could start getting to work. I used oak poles for the rafters and bark for the roof and shakes for the walls and hand-split boards for the interior stuff. Then I split off the fence pickets for the garden and animal corral. Each one of them fences was almost a month of work. But for being all the way up here and having no other way of doing it, it was easier for me to do that than carry up a whole roll of chicken wire. Plus, I was on the trip of trying to get it all together anyway. We were just trying to interchange as many natural functions for the ones that you go out and buy—a broom made out of a bush, making the stove out of junk, just as many reverse trips as you could think of. The stove stuff I got from the dump. The only thing we paid for was the nails. We didn't even need hinges, 'cause the windows didn't open and we didn't have any doors. The door was your ventilation—one on each side plus a hole in the roof in the summertime. I didn't want a door—I figured a door kept you locked out from the world. I was on this trip where I wanted to get to know the animals as much as possible, so if you have a door the animals aren't gonna come in. As it was, we'd have every day seven or eight chipmunks in there all day long; you could just sit on the bed and watch the chipmunks going back and forth. And mice, but the mice were kept in check by those wild cats that would come around. Ring-tailed cats. Used to be two or three of 'em would come in when we cooked up meat for dinner. We'd sit at the table and eat and just be real still and quiet, and they'd walk right up on the table and eat out of the pan right alongside of us. At night they'd be all around the place; they'd walk right across the goddam bed sometimes. At some points they started scaring me. Of course, in the meantime they were also gobbling all our chickens at an incredible rate. I guess I wanted to have the cats around more than I wanted the chickens at that point. That was a treat and a half: you weren't ever even supposed to see those things, and here they were coming to our house. But they stopped coming when we started driving in. I've never seen one since.

Back then we were living on practically nothing, that's for sure. We had a hundred-pound sack of brown rice we'd carry up here, fifty-pound bags of flour. We weren't eating enough, which got to me. That was one of the reasons I got off the trip right there—I could tell that my body was getting fucked up from not getting enough protein. Mostly just brown rice; a lot of times we were even lucky to have onions to stick in it. Soy sauce, soy beans; occasional venison, salmon, or squirrel—usually what people gave me, because at that point in my life I didn't want to go kill anything myself. We used to drink a lot of pine-needle tea, yerba-buena tea. But still, we just didn't eat good enough.

That's when I began to realize that I'd have to get some kind of money trip together. I was just hoping I could get along without money as much as possible, or get some kind of creative hustle on the side. But then I started to utilize the wood on the land for money. People kept asking me for fence posts. In the process of getting my own trip together, I learned how to work with redwood, so then other people started approaching me for split stuff, 'cause they didn't know where the hell to get it from. But I still had the basic problem that I was walking in and out of there, so there was no real way to take it out. I had to put it on a wagon and roll it down old logging roads, fence posts on a wagon for three quarters of a mile and then carry the wagon all the way back up. All I made was thirty bucks, and that was enough of that.

But after Mary left, that's when I really realized I needed to have an income, 'cause she was getting a little bit of money from her parents. So I started cutting those shingle bolts. That's when

I really started doing it for money, and that was just terrible. Don and I, we'd work about five heavy hours, in a sweat the whole time, and each make about ten bucks. It's not quite as bad as cutting firewood by the cord for sale—it's just one step above that. But I still consider it about the most basic trip.

The supply was the problem with split stuff, 'cause you have to have perfectly clear wood But I saw doing that that there was all this other wood lying around, all these old knotty logs that nobody had any use for at all. So I started freehand cutting slabs with my chain saw, cutting them off rough, but using real pretty wood, wood that had strange shapes, stuff that I figured I could sell down in the city.

That worked half successfully. I made enough money selling slabs to get the Alaskan mill together. And that thing just made a huge difference. Immediately everything became easy. It was rigged to cut slabs perfectly, real evenly—you didn't have to do it all freehand. All it is is just a chain saw on roller bars; it just slides along. But you really need good equipment like that, especially working in the woods, where you have to fight all those natural elements anyway.

Once I got into slabs, I never had any problem with supply. It's just incredible how much wood there is lying around. In the structure of a logging operation, they'll take a piece of land and they'll send in a crew of guys to cut the trees down. Now the guys who drag the logs out are a whole separate crew—they can't be working together or they're gonna get squashed. So it's the choke setter's job to go in there and find all the trees that were cut down, which can be a difficult job, and the choke setter, if he's having a really bad day, will just overlook a little section of woods, depending on his relation to his boss. In the case of this particular land here, that for a fact happened. My neighbor talked to the crew that logged it, and they said they were really uptight—it was late fall, and all their equipment was breaking down. They told the owner they'd rather wait until spring to pull the logs out, but he said no, he wanted the job done right away. So they went in there and just took all the surface logs, the logs right along the side of the road that the owner could see right off the bat. All the rest, they left. So that piece of land is just covered with wood, huge perfect logs they just didn't bother to pull.

Another place I found, it was just a case of oversight. There was some brush in the front near the road, then all of a sudden there was just a whole forest that had been logged off and was just sitting there. Twelve beautiful trees—they never got one of them out.

Then aside from that, they always had to leave any logs that are cracked, and anything that has a lot of knots in it. To begin with, they had all the trees in the world to choose from, so the mills would only take the good, perfectly clear wood. I used to be appalled by the amount of waste, but I can't be too appalled now, 'cause I can support myself for years on that amount of waste. It all *will* get used, 'cause there's nothing in the way of redwood that's gonna be wasted—the stuff will stay there practically forever and just not rot.

In all this time, I've only cut down two live redwoods. Just the direct bad karma of the operation pretty much discouraged me: the fear of felling something that weighed twenty or thirty tons, and controlling the fall so you didn't ruin it in the first place. Then when you got done with that, it's much more difficult to cut up because of the bark and all the slash of the branches and stuff. And it's a lot less useful 'cause it's all full of sap and green—it should be seasoned a couple of years. Plus, there's just not that many of them around anyway. Now, salvage wood, that's another matter. There's more than I could hope to use.

But my trouble is now that too many people have seen how good the trip is and have moved into the area. The market has always been limited anyway—how many people are gonna buy fancy wood? In Briceland there's two or three people that have tons of wood, more wood than they can sell, and in Garberville, in Redway, in every town going north and every town going south there's people doing the same trip. There's plenty of wood, but making the fancy wood for tables, and unique building wood, there's just not that much of a market for. For me, it's more like a hobby right now as far as the money it brings in. It keeps me alive, as it always has, but it's getting worse as time goes on instead of better as far as sales go.

Of course, the salvage wood can also be used for lumber pretty successfully. If more people get into that, there'll be a little bit of a market there. Salvage logging should take on a much more important aspect as time goes on. But the logs will mostly be pulled out and sawn by regular sawmills into lumber. Just last year, the mills started buying wood that was already on the ground; before that, they wouldn't touch it. I don't have the money to do that on any kind of scale. You need a Cat to pull the logs out, and a loading truck. And cutting it yourself, even with an Alaskan mill, doesn't give you as smooth a cut on the lumber. There'll be a degree of fluctuation—a four-by-eight board on one end might be three and three quarters by seven and three quarters on the other. I don't feel safe enough in the regular market, but now what I've done is reduced my price on beams that I can have a little sloppy. For general funky building, a good strong chunk of wood, it's worth it. So I might be able to capture a little bit of a market in that direction. I've got a little additional mill now that cuts perpendicular, and that makes the whole trip easier. So I'm looking for business now for that kind of lumber, plus I'm able to mill all the wood I'm using for the new addition to my house.

Now, I'd do almost anything that anybody wanted me to for money. A month ago I had no money from slab sales—just *none* —and a guy was buying shingle bolts, so I started cutting shingle bolts. But that was just a crime, 'cause I'd take a log that'd be worth two hundred fifty dollars in slabs; I'd cut it up into shake bolts and get fifty dollars and have a huge pile of waste fire-wood. Anytime you work with split stuff, you're taking a round log and turning it into a bunch of things that are square, so you end up with all these triangular pieces. Then every time you get a knot, you've got to throw that part away. It's a wasteful oper-ation. I didn't even want to do it, but I had to, 'cause that was the only cash market. I'd almost rather cut firewood up, 'cause then you aren't wasting good wood. It'll take another two thou-sand years to get 'em back to logs like I'm using right now. With a slab, you don't waste anything, you take it right out to the bark. The only thing you lose there is just the sawdust.

But I've got to get my trip more together on the homestead, too. If things get as bad as people say, I'm going to have this forty acres and all the land around it, and that's going to be supplying everything I need, pretty much. Certainly, being so remote as I am now and the way gasoline is going up in price, I'm gonna be spending more and more time here all the time, 'cause I just can't afford to go out. I can't hardly afford to go out the end of my road—you drive in low gear and you use at least a couple gallons of gas, damn near a buck. And lotta times I'm living on ten bucks a week even now. I worked it out that I made seventeen hundred dollars last year on my slabs, which is more than I ever made before, but I bet I could damn near come up with seventeen hundred dollars' worth of mechanical expenses and drums of gasoline. Now there's other little hustles here and there, like I'll sell a painting or something. My problem is that I'm not really willing to dedicate myself to any one pursuit. I want to be a painter and a musician, but neither one of those pays anything, so I have to cut wood to make the money in order to stay alive in order to paint and play music and just hang out. I'm not willing to put in eight hours a day five days a week to go to L.A. and San Francisco hustling the wood to make a real good business out of it. I'm Mickey-Mousing it, which is dangerous, but I like my independence. So I just have wood as a sideline, a half a hobby which brings in a few bucks. And actually it isn't much more than a natural outgrowth of an organic homestead. You're taking what your piece of land happens to give you. I just looked around at what I had a plentiful supply of, which is wood. I knew that it was something that could be sold, so I got the tools together, whatever it took to make it work. Now, if the business dies, I've still got the tools. I've already built several houses, and I could build any number more with the amount of salvage wood I have around here.

What Mark and others are just now learning is that the wealth of mainstream society is not quite so immense as it appeared a few years back, that to base one's livelihood on providing luxury items for the well-to-do plugs him into an economy with which, ultimately, he does not wish to remain involved. Instead, he would do better to produce something with a more utilitarian and universal appeal—just plain lumber, for instance, or some item made of wood that people really need and can readily afford. Homesteaders who had hoped to get by on crafts are slowly changing their minds and entering other, more practical fields. Many, for instance, have taken up commercial fishing as a way to make a living off the resources they find near their homes. To fish in the ocean, however, one needs a decent boat, and the fishermen often find themselves caught in the spiral of advancing technology; they must constantly be earning enough money to invest in better, safer equipment.

Indeed, the new agrarian movement is scarcely a decade old, yet already the homesteaders' technology—and their society—seems to be less primitive, more in tune with the modern-day world. There is an increasing level of comfort and convenience in their homes as people come to realize that hot water does indeed clean better than cold, that electric light is cleaner than gas. There is more attention being paid to the traditional local politics of taxes and schools as the homesteaders begin to take their place in the world at large. And there is even an increasing interest in the business community as a few of the rural émigrés open up grocery stores, shoe-repair shops, and pizza parlors in the small towns that service their homes.

The homesteaders, in a word, are rediscovering the world as they re-create it themselves on a smaller, more human scale. Now they know where food and shelter come from—and human society, too. And they know, or are learning, how to subsist on a used-up countryside by perfecting the art of scrounging and scraping by.

10

No Place Like Home

On a dark, bleak day in February, John was walking home from the dwelling place of Saul and Anon, his neighbors on the Mid-Mountain Ranch. The hilly dirt road was deeply rutted by the rains; the nearest paved road was several miles away. Upon arriving at his one-room cabin, John was greeted by two block-lettered posters hanging conspicuously on the doorway: "No-TICE TO THE PUBLIC," announced the first, although the public was nowhere in sight. "These premises have been found to be UNFIT FOR HUMAN HABITATION OR OCCUPANCY and are required to be and remain VACATED." The second bore a similar message: "NOTICE. PROHIBITED OCCUPANCY. This building is unfit for human occupancy and shall not be occupied until approved by this department as complying with state law." The posters were signed by the Mendocino County Health Department and the Department of Building Inspector, respectively. John's house had been "tagged."

There was additional evidence that an inspection had been made. "They had obviously come in," says John, "because I have a no-shoe policy, and there were dirty boot marks all over my rug." John spent that night at home, but the next morning he went away to the city, trying to figure out what to do. Should he just move on? Forget this life and try to set up elsewhere? No, that was impossible. He was a landowner now, and this was his home. "I came to the conclusion that I have to stay up here, 'cause this is where I live."

Brent, John's friend and land partner, was at home when the

inspectors arrived. "It was a cold and foggy winter day," he says, "and I was laying up in my bed and I was reading. All of a sudden, the hair set up on the back of my neck and I just knew something wasn't right. I turned around and looked, and there's these three guys out there with briefcases and note pads, looking at my house and taking notes. I went out there, and they introduced themselves: they were from the Building Department and the Health Department. And they were just writing away, and writing away, and every now and again they'd ask me some questions, like was it my land and stuff like that. Then they took these tags out. White tags about this big. One of 'em says: 'Notice to the public. Unfit for human occupancy.' And the other one is about the same. So they hung up the tags and went back and were standing around, and I asked them: 'What do you expect of me?' I figured that they'd give me some long rap about how I could bring it up to code. But they really surprised me. They said, 'You're going to have to tear it down.' They took their briefcases and walked off into the fog."

A week later, Brent received a letter in the mail: "The structures are in violation of the Mendocino County Building, Zoning and Health Codes and must be vacated and demolished immediately. If demolition is not completed by March 22, 1974, we will have no recourse except to take formal action as set forth in the applicable codes." It seemed that Brent and his partner, John, had thirty days to dismantle their houses, or else the county would do the wrecking for them. If they failed to comply, they each could be found guilty of a misdemeanor and sentenced to six months in jail and a $500 fine—just for continuing to live in the cabins that they themselves had built.

The inspectors undoubtedly had little difficulty in determining that Brent's ten-by-twelve-foot cabin was not up to code. The well-weathered wood came from an old barn, while the wooden-sash windows had been thrown away by people who were replacing them with aluminum frames. Four-foot-square rubber floor mats, also obtained free, were patched together to form a watertight seal to the roof, while the foundation posts had been taken from the surrounding pine forest, which Brent had selectively thinned. Only the nails and the stovepipe were newly purchased; the entire structure was put together for a mere twenty-five dollars.

Try as they might, the inspectors could not find any provisions in the multi-volume Uniform Building Code dealing with the use of rubber floor mats on the roof. The people who write the regulations simply don't think in those terms. The U.B.C., in force throughout the state of California, is drawn up by the International Conference of Building Inspectors; the building inspectors themselves are generally required to have some experience as contractors. It is only natural, therefore, that the code reflects the thinking of professional contractors and refers to the types of buildings that are generally constructed on a professional scale. There are complicated charts of stresses and strains, and requirements for specified types of building materials. Among other things, the codes lay down the rules for a full-perimeter foundation, wall studs every sixteen inches, a bathroom complete with sink, toilet, and shower or tub, hot and cold running water under forty pounds of pressure, minimum room sizes and ceiling heights, and 70-degree heat throughout the house. Provisions are included for alternative structures, but any building deviating from the specific requirements of the code—such as Brent's cabin, with its unique weatherproofing materials—must be approved by a licensed civil engineer at the expense of the builder.

Ideally, the building codes are a form of consumer protection. By specifying minimum standards concerning the quality of materials and the engineering of the house, the codes can guarantee to untutored buyers that the homes they purchase will be structurally safe and sound. But what of the person who wishes to construct his own shelter? Should he, too, be bound by the provisions of the codes?

There is a strong element of traditional conservatism here in Mendocino County, as there is elsewhere in rural America, that still believes in the basic tenet "A man's home is his castle." If you want to build yourself a house, say the old-timers, you have every right to do it—and to do it however you damn well please. But now the codes tell them they can't, that they have to do it thus and so: "Can't even build a goddamn chicken house no more without them saying it's okay," says an embittered old-timer named Frank.

But it is not the older folks whose houses are being condemned. Brent and John are not yet thirty years of age. Like many of their neighbors, they have moved from the cities to the countryside in order to establish a life more closely linked to the fundamentals of survival. They are, in short, part of the new breed of rural folk, self-styled homesteaders, who for reasons of ecology and economics often wish to build lightweight houses which use a minimum of materials; who rarely wish to construct rectangular, framed dwellings with full-perimeter foundations, flush toilets, and central heating. They are interested in building with recycled materials and/or milling their own lumber, and in devising new methods of sanitation.

It is little wonder, therefore, that they have come into conflict with the more standardized codes of modern society. Just as rubber floor mats on the roof are a totally alien concept to the inspectors, so too do the terms of the building codes seem foreign to the new pioneers. The fee for a building permit, for instance, is figured on the basis of the square footage in each of four categories: "floor area," "garage," "carport," and "deck awning." Brent and John think more in terms of chicken coops and woodsheds than carports and deck awnings, and they naturally feel a bit out of place when being judged by a set of rules established primarily by and for the urban and suburban worlds they have left behind.

Donald Uhr, chief building inspector for Mendocino County, has little admiration for the young homesteaders and their way of life. "Hell," he says, "let's not revert *back* in time. I grew up back in the plains of Nebraska, and I knew what it was to get up in the middle of the night and trot out through the goddam snow to the outdoor privy. And I don't see where that's *living* in any way, shape, or form. That's where I differentiate from their thinking and lifestyle." The differences are understandable: Uhr wants the luxuries he was deprived of as a child, while the back-to-the-land people are seeking an elemental simplicity which has been lacking in their lives. Yet the situation is not symmetrical, for it is Uhr who has the power to enforce the codes, and the codes have been written in the context of the modernized world he has come to accept—but which the homesteaders have not.

The back-to-the-landers, however, are not as powerless as at first it might seem. Unlike the original homesteaders of generations past, the new pioneers have grown up with a certain political consciousness which is unique to the twentieth century: if something strikes them as wrong, they know how to organize, how to lobby, and how to use public relations techniques in order to set things right. They are not about to sit idly by while their houses are torn to the ground. If the laws are too restrictive, these idealistic young settlers feel they might be able to change them.

"I spent the whole next day," says Brent, "just laying in bed and thinking about it: whose house I could blow up and burn down in retaliation. But I realized that if I made the decision to do those sorts of things, then I'd have to live with the consequences. Violence breeds violence. But something had to be done, so I went down to Saul and Anon's and we sat around and rapped about it."

Saul and Anon's house had not itself been tagged, but they felt and acted as if it had. They had both worked as weavers for twelve hours a day in order to get enough money to meet the down payment on their land and to erect a simple shelter; they were not about to sit back and wait for the inspectors to pay them a personal visit. "We had to get away," says Anon. "Sitting in our homes was incredible—we could envision hearing the bulldozer. We didn't know what our rights were, we didn't know where we stood. We knew that we were illegal, and we knew that *we* were being fingered, not just our structures. Where's this at, where you can't move onto your own land and build your own house, and you don't hurt anybody around you? We've been saying that for a long time, and then some of us got tagged and we suddenly decided: Gadzooks, we got thirty days to tear down our houses—or else do something about it."

"From there," says Brent, "we just started a campaign, going around the county and telling folks about it. Everywhere we went it was incredible, because it was people's *homes*. That's the neat part of the whole thing. If anybody's got land, or even thinking about getting land or building a house, they're *automatically* involved. It's an issue that goes right to the heart. It's just basic: where are you gonna live?"

Backcountry homeowners from around the county were quick to jump on the bandwagon which Brent, John, Saul, and Anon had launched. The movement soon took on a name—United Stand—and grass-roots meetings were held throughout the hills, at which the modern-day homesteaders voiced their dissatisfaction with the governmental bureaucracy that had so suddenly forced its way into their lives.

A few of the young homesteaders had dabbled in politics before, but this was an altogether new experience even for them. No longer were they campus radicals, and this time the issue was not some abstract ideal: the issue was themselves. "I've worn my feet to stubs for civil rights," says Anon, "but I've never been black or Chicano. But I *am* a homeowner."

It made no sense to run a political movement from off in the hills, and so, ironically, several of the organizers had to abandon their new-found homesteads, at least for the time being, and move into town. They rented a small apartment in Ukiah (the Mendocino County seat), converted a corner of the kitchen into an office, and set up shop. Some of the chairs had no backs, the legs were falling off the tables, the traffic from the main drag roared outside their window—but for a while it would have to do. They rediscovered the beauty and efficiency of the three-by-five index card; they resurrected an old ditto machine and put out a newsletter; they issued press releases and made appointments with local politicians. Just as they once tried to approach self-sufficiency on the land, so too did they aspire toward self-sufficiency in their current project: "The approach we take," says Brent, who has suddenly become knowledgeable in legal matters, "is to do nearly everything we can ourselves. So I opened the books and got into law."

"It's a natural extension of our lifestyle," adds John. "We

move into the country and look around and see how we can get along with the ecosystem. Now we move back into town and see how we can get along with the political system that's already there."

But the political system that was already there has turned out to be even more complex and problematical than they had anticipated. There are no fewer than six separate governmental bodies with whom they must deal if they ever hope to move back into their houses on a legal basis: the Office of Building Inspector, the Health Department, the Planning Department, the District Attorney's office, the Mendocino County Board of Supervisors, and the State Legislature.

In order for the owners of tagged houses to obtain a building permit, they would first have to pay a double fee (and, of course, they would have to hope that the D.A.'s office would agree not to prosecute them for the misdemeanor of building without a permit in the first place). They would also have to take the application for a permit over to the Planning Department to make sure their proposed building was consistent with county zoning policies and that it was not situated on an illegal land division. The problem, however, is that many of the tagged houses *are* situated on illegal land divisions—a fact that the owners have only recently discovered. At fault are the speculators and realtors who sold them their land, but the potential homesteaders are forbidden to pursue their application for a building permit until the original owners clear up matters with the Planning Department. This might take months or it might take years; meanwhile, there is no way the new owners can legally build on their land. They do have civil recourse—that is, they could sue the people who sold them their parcels—but that's not the point. They don't want the money, they want the right to live on the land they thought they had bought.

If and when the problem of land division is straightened out, the new homesteaders will have to confront the Planning Department with yet another question: How many dwellings are allowed on a parcel? Presently, only one living unit is permitted on each legally recognized division of land. But many of the parcels have been bought in partnerships, and the partners rarely show any interest in dividing up the land still further so that they each could have their own separate pieces upon which to build. They feel there are already too many artificial lines segmenting the landscape—and they don't wish to make the situation any worse.

Once the Planning Department has given its stamp of approval, an application for a building permit must then be signed by the Health Department, which is interested primarily in waste disposal. Traditionally, the only acceptable method of waste disposal in areas not serviced by a sewer system has been the septic tank. But these large underground bins with their accompanying leach fields are ill suited to the realities of low-economic-level backcountry homesteads: they are expensive to construct, often costing more than the houses themselves; they require large amounts of water, often more than can be spared on the marginal land inhabited by the new pioneers; the hardpan earth in the backhills can make effective leaching an impossibility, resulting in surface exposure of human wastes. Then there is also the problem of philosophy: in the septic-tank system, human waste is not recycled. This, to the folks at United Stand, is its most basic shortcoming: "We want to follow through on the consequences of our daily lives," says Brent. "What scares me most about septic tanks is that it's supposed to just go away. But I *know* it doesn't just go away."

United Stand's alternative solution to the problem of waste disposal is the compost privy. Cheaper to construct than a septic-tank system, a compost privy requires no water and no leach field, and yet, in approximately one year, it turns human waste into effective, disease-free fertilizer. Although it is extensively used in other countries, the compost privy seems to contradict the basic tenet of waste disposal in America: to get rid of the darn stuff, to wash one's hands clean. The County Health Department is thus hesitant to give official sanction to the recycling of human excrement, and as the political battle rages on in Ukiah, most of the homesteaders back in the hills continue to use only the tried and true: the old-fashioned outhouse.

Finally, if the Planning Department and the Health Department somehow grant their approval, the application for a building permit is forwarded to the Building Department itself. Yet even should the building inspector approve the blueprints, there remains the problem of where the homesteaders will live while they do the work on their houses. They often construct small, one-room cabins which serve as "home" for the first year or two, but many of these temporary dwellings have themselves been tagged—thus leaving the homesteaders with no base from which to operate. The only temporary structure with any legal standing, according to building inspector Don Uhr, is "a construction shack that the contractor puts up while he's on the job." Such "shacks" are not to be lived in, and Uhr, who believes in upholding both the letter and the spirit of the law, is unlikely to show much leniency toward any transgressors. "Hell," he says, "they give us the codes and we're going to enforce them. The days of immunity for the building inspector are over. Like this house falling off a bluff—this was up for thirty years, and it just fell down. If they could have related this to some building inspector, he would have gotten sued."

Don Uhr, like the codes he is entrusted to administer, sees building primarily as an activity reserved for contractors. When I asked him about the question of owner-built housing, his response was quick: "What building isn't owner-built? The contractor owns the building until he sells it to someone else, so it's owner-built."

"Well, then 'dweller-built' or something like that."

"Yeah, you're talking about a *contracted* home."

"I'm talking about somebody who owns a piece of land and wants to build a house on it, and does the work himself."

"Here again, you can see the contractors' position. If Joe Blow would be allowed to build and use subgraded materials and build a substandard house, he has to compete—and this is his living—and this guy can turn around and sell that house."

Perhaps, but that's not what the new homesteaders are all about. They aren't in it for the money; they want to build their own houses and live in them themselves. In many cases, they wish to mill their own lumber, but this too is seen by Uhr—and by the law—in terms of buying and selling: "Here again, if they come out of a mill, they're getting into a category of merchandising material that is regulated."

There is a definite irony in all this: the back-to-the-land folks want only to do what mankind has done for thousands and thousands of years—to build their own dwellings. Yet somehow this comes across today as a radical idea, for people just don't do that sort of thing any more. Houses are what contractors build; if you build your own, then you, too, are seen as a contractor. A letter to the *Mendocino Beacon* argued indignantly against the people represented by United Stand: "Whether it be one person building 100 homes or 100 persons building one home each, we are dealing with *Developers*—regardless of self-serving statements of belief, morality, purpose, fantasy and delusions."

But for the people involved in the new agrarian movement, there *is* a difference, and it is one of quality as well as quantity. To build one's own shelter is seen as one of the most positive experiences that life has to offer. "I've never owned a home before," says Marie, who might get rather angry if anyone ever called her a "developer" to her face. "I've always rented places. The thing I like about owning a home is just to do things my way. In rented houses you can't hang up pictures 'cause it's gonna make a little hole in the wall. You can't have things your way. I've *liked* places I've rented a lot, but I've never *loved* them. I've never just looked all around and seen all kinds of things that I made—like I made those drawers, and my little latch on the door that closes just right, and my macrame handles. I couldn't see building a house and making it look just like all the houses that I rented, or building a house just by somebody's exact code. I really don't know if my door latch is code, but it is macrame and it has beads and I love the way it latches when you go in and out. It just wouldn't be any fun to go to the hardware store and order the code latch and put it on my door."

If the new homesteaders moved to the countryside in order to simplify their lives, the end result has been quite the reverse: they are confronted with an awesome array of rules, regulations, and bureaucracies that can no longer be ignored. In order to proceed with the simple business of building their houses, they must in many cases wait for their land divisions to be made legal; they must change the law that permits only one dwelling to a parcel; they must find alternative methods of waste disposal which are acceptable both to themselves and to county officials; they must find a way to live legally on their land while they build; they must modify the building codes to make room for their lightweight, unconventional structures. The various issues are not separate, but related. If the homesteaders somehow managed to gain acceptance from the Health Department for their compost privies, for instance, the Building Department could still require the presence of a flush toilet—whether it is connected with plumbing or not.

This, then, is what our government has become: a labyrinth of restrictions that present obstacles to the citizens at every turn. What ever happened to the idea that the government exists first and foremost to serve the interests of the people? "I was raised in Arkansas until I was twelve years old," recalls Earl Hall, a resident of Fort Bragg who moved to California back in the 1930's. "We lived on a farm. As far as I know, there were only two people in government that ever came around. One was a man and his function was kind of all-around adviser. He could advise you on how to remedy almost any problem from a stinking outhouse to the cure of any ailing animal. We would see him about twice a year and he would send a notice by mail about the time he would be around. The other was a woman and her function was as a demonstrator and adviser. She would pick a house with a large kitchen and a large dining room and she would demonstrate the latest method of canning and preserving foods. All the neighboring women who wanted to would come and spend the day. We saw her about once a year. Both these people were well versed on health and sanitation. People were eager to see them come around, as they came as a helpful friend. There was no fear that these people would red-tag a house or harass anyone. They gave their advice freely, you could take it or not. The choice was *yours*."

Earl Hall is not a "new homesteader." A member of an older generation, he has tackled the problem of shelter somewhat differently: he and his family live in a trailer rather than a hand-made house. But both Earl Hall and United Stand find themselves in the same predicament: neither can afford to build and pay taxes on a code house. And so Earl Hall, like his younger counterparts, has taken his stand in the face of governmental authority. "Take the noose from around our necks and we will build better homes and better farm buildings. Take the shackles off and let the people build what they want and you might be surprised at how good they are at it. Do away with the policing departments and give us an advisory department that we don't have to be afraid of and we will do a good job. Maybe the code is good for policing the contractor so he doesn't cheat anyone. However, it is not needed for the man who wants to build his own, for he has no reason to cheat himself. Most of the people I know are afraid to speak up on this issue for fear of harassment. They fear they have too much to lose and have no hope that they would get any satisfaction. Is this the relationship the government wants?"

The people represented by United Stand are challenging the pliability and adaptability of "the System." Is there room for their anachronistic ways in the modern world? As far as the new homesteaders are concerned, the net effect of the building codes is to enforce standardization and conformity with commonly accepted styles. "I think I understand," says Marie, "where their sense of wanting to regulate things comes from. It reminds me of when I taught seventh-grade black kids in South Carolina who were about to go into integrated schools. They're coming in from the countryside, they're black, and they're saying 'ain't' and they're speaking in this dialect which is in fact very, very colorful. But I was supposed to teach them grammar, so I had to knock out their 'ain'ts' and I had to knock out all the very picturesque, individualized speech and try to get them to conform to these rules and regulations which didn't have a whole lot to say about *them*. And I had dual feelings about it, because I realized that they had to conform in some ways to make it, but I also realized that I was really cutting them down to size. I feel the same thing is happening with us. There are people out there, and rules and regulations out there, which in some ways make a kind of sense, just like grammar makes sense. But in some ways it's very outrageous. It takes away people's individuality. I think what's happening to us is what's happening to a lot of people in this country. You have a mainstream culture, which is fine, but what's bad about it is when it's applied to little black kids in South Carolina, or to people who have incredibly beautiful, individualized, comfortable homes. The culture should be growing bigger to give more individuals more space. It's like black culture, or Orientals who want their culture accepted, or Spanish-speaking people who want *their* culture accepted—and now it's *rural* culture. Unless the country can go that way and be flexible enough to be inclusive rather than exclusive, you're just going to get an incredibly monotonous world."

Just as blacks, Orientals, and Chicanos have entered the political arena to demand what they feel is rightfully theirs, so too are these converts to rural lifestyles now organizing to seek a space for themselves. United Stand has taken its case before the County Board of Supervisors, which responded in typical fashion by setting up a committee to study the problem. Yet Mendocino is still very much of a rural county, and the concern on the part of the supervisors for the problems of rural folk seems genuine. Supervisor Augie Avila, for instance, has little difficulty relating to the problem at hand: "Maybe some of the standards that are set forth are not necessarily required in remote areas. I don't see that we have to have a full cement foundation. I have two-by-fours in my home that are *measured* two-by-fours. You buy a two-by-four today, and you wonder *what* they are."

According to the State Housing Code, the Board of Supervisors of each county has the power to "make such changes or modifications in the requirements . . . as it determines are reasonably necessary because of local conditions." But just what are the "local conditions" that might justify modification of the building codes? In the Sierras, stronger roofs are required to bear the extra weight of the snow; in the Southland, insulation requirements might be lessened. But here in Mendocino County, it is not the weather that is special—it is the needs and desires of the people. There is a strong demand for low-cost, ecologically sound housing in areas of low population density; the problem lies in how to translate that demand into legal terms. Perhaps the law could focus on the rugged, inaccessible terrain inhabited by the homesteaders, or it might even take heed of the socioeconomic factors involved. United Stand's preferred solution is to create an altogether new class of "mountain cabins" which would be sanctioned by law. But county officials, even if sympathetic, are scared to put themselves out on a limb by modifying state laws. It is thus likely that the case will eventually have to come before the State Legislature, at which point the powerful lobbyists for the building trades will undoubtedly exert considerable pressure to maintain the codes that they themselves created.

United Stand, in short, has a long way to go before many of its members can legally move back on their land. Even should they fail to change the codes, however, the existing laws will be hard to enforce. For each separate violation, all the administrative procedures have to be followed, including a hearing by the Board of Appeals. After that, each case must go through the courts, where the defendants are likely to raise a slew of questions ranging from constitutional issues to the legal technicalities of conducting a proper building inspection. Each case would have to be tried on its own merits, and since there are literally thousands of permit-less structures throughout the county, the time and energy it would require of the governmental machinery staggers the imagination of local officials and makes many of them almost as eager as United Stand to seek alternative solutions. "We can build houses faster than they can prosecute," says Rusty, a member of United Stand. "They'll never get us all. If they want safe, sanitary facilities, they're going to have to offer us something we can buy." The situation is reminiscent of Prohibition days—there are just too many people operating outside the scope of the law for the law to be truly effective. It is an unstable situation, and something—or someone—will have to give ground.

Although victory is by no means certain, the struggle itself has had some positive effects on its previously anarchistic participants. "Before, we were all hiding out in our own little worlds," says Anon. "We didn't want anybody to know anything. What this thing has done is not only get us in contact with the outside, but also with each other. We're all over the place, but we didn't know it before. It's a whole new nation. Now we know who we are. And we know if we don't hang together, we'll hang separately."

Anon's language sounds familiar: "If we don't hang together, we'll hang separately." That same line has been used by organizers of movements since the American Revolution—wherever and whenever people have banded together to seek what they thought was rightfully theirs. Here in Mendocino County it is the young radicals, many from urban backgrounds, who have banded together as the strongest advocates of a very traditional country conservatism. The situation is ironic indeed, and yet, ideologies and backgrounds aside, the issue is as basic as can be: Will they or won't they be allowed to lead their lives as they see fit? Can they or can't they build handmade houses in which they themselves will live? It is the archetypical battle of the Edges, with state laws requiring local people to conform to the standards set by and for the Metropolis. The particular circumstances of rural life have been ignored, and the idea that an individual can build his own home has been virtually negated by the law. Confronted by an awesome authority which has the power to enforce uniformity, the back-to-the-land folks have countered with a simple but persuasive argument based on the old-fashioned American belief in the rights of the individual: We have gone out of our way to stay out of your way. We have bought land that was not being used, placing little drain on the limited resources of the earth. We live simply and cheaply, consuming no more than our share. We interfere with no one, nor with the natural world. If we can't live thus, then what *are* we expected to do?

Part Five

THREATS
TO THE EDGES:
RECREATION AND
DEVELOPMENT

If you're writing a book of advice for people, it's that you have to keep your eyes and ears open for everything that these different departments do, and when something comes across your vision that looks funny, you're going to have to start on it *right then*, because by the time it starts making its way from the back page of the papers to the front, you're going to be lost. It'll be a *fait accompli:* "We've already spent all this money," they'll tell you. "How can we justify spending all this money unless we go ahead and build the dam, or put in the freeway?" It's really like playing chess. There's a certain amount of space on this board, and a certain number of rules that you operate by, simply because you are a human being. Someone else announces that they have certain designs on the chessboard, and you just have to keep track of their moves—and be very careful. You watch everything they're doing, because they're going to be watching everything you do.

—PHILIP STARR,
AN OPPONENT OF THE WHITETHORN DAM

II

The City That Is Not

THE PLASTER-OF-PARIS model of the Shelter Cove development, situated between the "Mermaids" and "Neptunes" rest rooms in the on-site sales office two hundred miles north of San Francisco, cost $7,000 to construct. Lights blink on and off in accompaniment to a dramatic narration which can be heard through any one of ten telephone receivers attatched to the model: "This wonderful place is called Shelter Cove Sea Park, California's finest recreational seacoast community unfolding between two worlds, the ocean-view spectacular and the park panorama, a master-planned sea-front wonderland coming to life." The background music is constantly swelling throughout the five-minute broadcast.

A list of recent sales covers one of the walls, stating the buyers' names and addresses: Los Angeles, Las Vegas, Belgium, Germany. Outside the office, overlooking the scenic shoreline bluffs, are a horseshoe pit and a putting green. And just beyond, a 3,400-foot paved runway (which the company proudly announces ran them half a million dollars) stretches into the ocean. During the periods of peak sales activity several years ago, ninety-six prospective buyers were flown up from L.A. each weekend on three separate airplanes.

Shelter Cove Sea Park is built on the scale of a small city. There are 4,600 lots serviced by forty-three miles of paved roads and complete water, sewage, and electrical facilities. Roadside signs take interested parties through a "Discovery Tour" of the development's highlights, leading past billboards which boast

163

of the developers' technical achievements: "Discovery Tour 7—Sewage Treatment Plant. All sewage flows into this plant via 24 miles of pipe and 9 pump stations. It goes through a communitor (grinder), controlled aeration tank, sedimentation tank, where chlorine is added, and a holding pond before entering an outfall pipe leading to the ocean."

Shelter Cove seems to have everything—everything, that is, except people. Over 4,400 lots have been sold, yet only thirty houses are built, and not all of those are lived in. The development has been in operation for almost a decade, and it's been over five years since the major facilities were completed. Why, then, does nobody live here?

That's a touchy point with the company spokesmen, who alternately blame political problems with Humboldt County and point to figures of how many people plan to build homes in the near future. Resident sales manager Jim Dawson feels that people will start building soon, now that the county has agreed to pick up the tab for maintaining the roads. But some of the would-be residents feel the problem is not so simple. They point to inflation in the building trades and to increasingly high interest rates. "It's hard to get financing out here," says a landowner —as if it weren't hard everywhere. Then there's always the Coastal Commission to blame, for the Shelter Cove development now falls under its jurisdiction. One early buyer, who has since sold his land, points to the twenty-five miles of narrow, winding roads which must be traversed to reach Shelter Cove from Highway 101, while a prospective homeowner claims that he would like to build a house—if only he could find a contractor willing to undertake the job out there in the boondocks. Some of the old-time locals, meanwhile, explain that an Indian chief put a curse on Shelter Cove after some of his people had been massacred there.

Perhaps the most reasonable explanation for the lack of residents is that at least half of the purchasers were speculators who never intended to live here in the first place. *The Beachcomber*, the company newspaper, suggestively quotes Will Rogers: "The way to make money in real estate is to find out where people are buying, and buy land before they get there!" And as for the nonspeculators, most of them probably purchased lots upon which they might someday (but not just yet) build their retirement homes. The promoters, indeed, give a special pitch toward future pensioners: "You are actually surrounded and protected from the entire world!" Proudly, they quote an anonymous settler in one of their brochures: "This is the end of the rainbow for us."

As a retirement community, Shelter Cove is faced with the problem of end-of-the-line boredom. Just what is there to do with oneself—particularly way out here in the middle of nowhere? The company points to its "professionally designed" nine-hole golf course and to the hunting and fishing opportunities nearby. *The Beachcomber*, using the strategy that a good offense is the best defense, is filled with stories of how this or that couple is "busier now than before retirement." Charleen Dawson, wife of the resident manager, tries to allay the fears of some of the future residents in her personalized column for the company paper:

One of the questions asked most frequently by visitors to Shelter Cove is "What is there to do—how do you fill your days?" Would that days were longer! There is a great deal of peace in living here—contentment is synonymous with Shelter Cove—but there is also some frustration, due to time slipping away so quickly.

Things to do—walking: on the roads, on the hills, on the beaches. Rocks to climb, driftwood to gather, birds and animals to watch. Just keeping a lookout for whales takes time!

Visiting neighbors is another pleasure; we are gaining new friends as each new home is completed. We all entertain a lot, and as so many of the women here are excellent cooks and bakers, some of us are becoming rather rotund. I walk quickly past the scales each morning—why ruin a new day with bad news?

We have our pot-luck dinners monthly, followed by bingo, or just talk. Some couples have weekly card parties. Pioneer meetings, Resort Improvement meetings, Coastal Commission meetings, take up many hours each month.

But most of the time is spent in pursuing personal hobbies and pleasures, crafts and arts. Needlework, crocheting, knitting, sewing, candlemaking, lapidary creations, tin-craft, painting, carpentering, model-making, mosaics, photography, gardening, coquillage, decoupage, string art, to name some of the avocations of our residents.

I leave the best, to my way of thinking, to the last—the joy of reading.

But what of those traditional activities of country folk of all ages: raising stock, growing vegetables, chopping wood, etc.? The hills surrounding Shelter Cove are filled with "retired" old-timers whose days need not be passed with makeshift hobbies—instead, they continue to function in the practical world. But the urbanized folks at Shelter Cove, finally relieved of their nine-to-five jobs, have a different orientation altogether. They do not live on homesteads but on vacation retreats. Who could imagine a chicken coop on those city-sized lots?

A handful of Shelter Cove residents, however, have managed to stay active in the workaday world. John Aldridge, for instance, has emerged from retirement to run the motel that he himself had helped to build. "Now I don't mean to boast or nothing," he says as we sit on the parking-lot steps, "but I'm the last fella from the original crew that's still around. I worked here about six years until the roads, the water plant, and everything was finished. I remember the day I got over here it started raining. This road coming in here then was just an old dirt, crooked road. I told myself that day, if I ever come out of this place alive, I'd never come back again. I offered an old boy that day twenty dollars to drive my pickup back outa here, 'cause I was scared to drive it out. Just a little old narrow, winding, muddy road. I kept telling the boss every thirty days I was gonna leave, I was gonna leave."

"What'd you work on?" I ask him.

"I worked on everything. Started out working as a mechanic. Worked on cars, tractors, Cats—even wound up on airplanes out here. Then after this thing was finished, I taken it over for the county. 'District,' they call it. 'District One.'

"But we moved on back to Woodland, and back to New Mexico, where I started from. We thought we was really gonna like it there. My wife was born there. Anyway, I fished all over that whole country and couldn't catch a fish and finally I told her: you better get ready, 'cause I'm going back to Shelter Cove. So we did, we come back out here. And a friend of mine lives over the mountain here, why he had a commercial license. First three days I was here I got fifteen salmon fishing with him.

"We really like it here," John continues. "There's just no other place in the world—and I've traveled the world over three or four times. There's nothing like Shelter Cove when it comes to the weather, the fishing. Well, it gets awful foggy at times, but then a coupla days later the sun'll come out like this. It's just really a swell place to live."

"Do you live here in the motel?"

"Yeah, I live here."

"You got a choice location here right by the sea."

"Well, if I had *my* choice, I would take it back up here on the hill a little further. I like the ocean, but I got more respect for the ocean than I have for anything in the world. I've seen a lot of 'em go since I been here. I was here when that big plane crash happened down there and killed all that bunch. Twenty-five of 'em, I think it was. And there was two that fell off the rocks right out here and both of them drownded. Two brothers fell in right back up here—both them drownded. There was one airplane crashed just over this knoll, too. Two men in it. Then about two years ago there was two kids come in here from up in Oregon or somewhere up in there and they lit in here and they went in and got gas and come back out and went to take off and shot right straight up and come right straight down. Killed both of *them*. Seen a lot of 'em come and go out here." Perhaps it was true—had the Indians really put a curse on the place?

"Was the big crash one of the planes coming up from L.A.?"

"Yeah, they was all salesmen, every one of them. Everyone that was on there was company men—company men and women."

"They had that many salesmen?"

"Oh, yeah. And that was just the ones that was working out here. There'd be thirty, forty at a time working out here on weekends. And they was flying people in and out here—bring 'em in early in the morning, keep 'em all day, feed 'em, and fly 'em out at night. They made a lotta sales that day, too. A whole suitcase full of money down in that ocean somewhere."

"What did the company do about getting more salesmen? That must have pretty much cleaned them out of their crew."

"Well, they had salesmen out here within a week. You take a town as big as that San Diego, L.A., and Frisco—they's hundreds of 'em down there that's looking for work. And at that time, they really had a sales program a-going here. But after that crash, it never really did take off here like it did before that."

"How much money do you think the corporation made on the whole thing?"

"That's probably out of my jurisdiction. I wouldn't even think about guessing at it. I don't have no idea whatsoever. I never have messed around with that, that's one thing I've stayed away from."

"Now that all the lots are sold, what's the company's position in it all? Do they have any further responsibility?"

"Shelter Cove?"

"Yeah."

"The best I can understand (you know, I was just one of the workingmen—I wasn't *supposed* to know anything and didn't know *too* much)—but they built all the roads, and the water plant, and the sewer plant, and all that kinda stuff; then they turned that over to the county. County taken the roads to maintain 'em, and Shelter Cove kept the lots. They sell and resell, people turns 'em back and they sell 'em again. Lotta these people, they bought these lots sight unseen. Then they come in here and a burnt buzzard couldn't light on their lots. And a lot of 'em comes in and, man, they've got a beautiful lot. There was a young couple, schoolteachers outta L.A., come in here two weeks ago. Wanted me to help find their lot. I don't know how them kids coulda been so lucky—they bought it off a dealer down there in San Diego, and they got one of the very choice lots in the whole place. Boy, it is a *beautiful* spot—I couldn't believe they could be that lucky buying one sight unseen. But then a colored guy came in, and he was from San Diego, too. That poor guy, I felt sorry for him. They didn't have enough room to even turn a car around up there—just straight off a cliff. But the company, they'll exchange it with 'em if they want. Leave 'em real satisfied. You might have to pay 'em a little money to boot, but they'll always trade you a good lot." Land, in short, has become a common commodity, sold over the counter like anything else. You don't have to homestead it, you don't have to live on it, you don't have to see it—all you have to do is buy it. Our Mother Earth is up for grabs.

The founders of the Shelter Cove Development Corporation were not the first ones to see the area's desirability as a place for human habitation. The Sinkyone Indians thrived on the game, acorns, and berries from the hillsides and the fish, mussels, and seaweed from the ocean. In the early 1850's, shortly after the rediscovery of Humboldt Bay seventy miles to the north, two men named Hamilton and Oliver came to graze their cattle and lay claim to the land. The Indians apparently hunted down the new game, which they found to be easy prey. Hamilton and Oliver became enraged. A quarrel with the Indians ensued and Oliver was killed. Hamilton then "sold" the land to the three Ray brothers. "The Ray brothers," says ninety-one-year-old Ernest McKee, whose father was one of the first settlers, "did the only sensible thing: they married Indian women and held the Shelter Cove Ranch."

More settlers followed, and in 1885 a wharf almost a thousand feet long was built out into the sheltered cove that gives the area its name. By the turn of the century, a minor industry had developed in the nearby hillsides: the bark from the tanbark oak tree was peeled and sent from the Shelter Cove wharf to processing plants along San Francisco Bay, where the tannic acids were removed for treating leather. The tanbark industry died out by the 1920's, but the wharf continued to service several hundred fishing boats which anchored in the cove each summer. The fishermen supported a fair-sized hotel where they could enjoy all the comforts of home. According to Ernest's cousin Lon McKee, who at one time ran the hotel, they were absolute suckers for lemon pie.

As logging activities caused the salmon population to dwindle by destroying the spawning beds in the rivers nearby, the fishing industry began to subside. The wharf fell apart in the 1930's and was never repaired. Today, only a handful of sport and commercial fishermen continue to use the cove, transporting themselves to and from their boats by small landing skiffs.

The Shelter Cove Ranch, meanwhile, became unprofitable. The land was too valuable, the taxes too high, to be used simply by sheep and cattle. The ranch was sold and then sold again until it finally wound up in the hands of the Shelter Cove Development Corporation. Basing themselves in Los Angeles, George Isaacs and R. J. Beaumont proceeded to direct one of the largest engineered developments on the Pacific Coast. The developers poured millions of dollars into carving the once majestic hillsides into an elaborate labyrinth of roadways. Rolling meadows formerly used for grazing were chopped into city-sized lots suitable for prefabricated vacation homes. The Shelter Cove countryside was thus transformed into an appendage of urbanized America almost overnight.

Shelter Cove would never be settled on a large-scale basis, however, unless all the amenities of life could be offered to the prospective homeowners. Water, sewage or septic tanks, electricity, and telephone service had to be made available to every lot. The entire substructure of this city-to-be thus had to be prepared in advance. But someone back in Los Angeles had the good fortune of rediscovering the old Municipal Improvement Act of 1913, and presto! Shelter Cove became its very own governmental unit (Resort Improvement District #1) which was not beholden to the county. Under this old law, which has since been stricken from the books, the company could undertake all the work itself, while using the District to level special assessments on the properties. The county government, which can often be a stickler in such construction projects, had no direct control over the quality of work being done.

But the developers hardly wanted to be the maintenance managers of their forty-three miles of paved roadway, complete with the accompanying drainage system, in perpetuity. They consequently entered into an agreement whereby the county would eventually take over the roads and the airport, while the rest of the utilities would still be managed by the Improvement District. But the county then insisted on certain standards for the roads—and there was considerable dispute over whether the developers had met these standards. Shelter Cove was consequently thrust into the forefront of local politics, with several grand jury reports devoted to the question of whether the county should or should not assume responsibility for all those suburban-looking streets. Finally, after the debate had raged for several years, the company paid the county a nominal fee and the roads were no longer theirs.

Behind the controversy over the roads lay differing attitudes concerning the development itself. When the project was first started in 1965, nearly everybody thought it was a great idea. It would increase the tax base dramatically and provide at least a handful of jobs. But as interest in conservation grew in the next few years, people began to see in the Shelter Cove project the destruction of one of few remaining enclaves of undeveloped coastal land. Do second-home communities, the conservationists asked, represent the most suitable use of our nation's contracting countryside? What impact will the fun-seeking newcomers have on the surrounding wilderness areas?

It's not only the ecology, but the politics as well. Shelter Cove has a potential population four times as large as any other town within a fifty-mile radius. What will happen when such a large group, consisting of people with basically urban and suburban backgrounds, is suddenly unleashed on the local scene? The Shelter Cove Development is a *fait accompli*, a ready-made product of twentieth-century America instantaneously transposed onto an alien, more primitive world. What will be the eventual effect upon the people and places of the Edges if and when the development is finally settled?

Or will that ever come to pass? Will a city someday spring up, as planned, in this "seaside haven"? Will the people ever move onto their vacant lots? Will Safeway and Shell signs soon be visible to the fishermen offshore?

At least for the moment, the backcountry has held Shelter Cove Sea Park to a standstill. Hardly anyone seems to want to

12

Grapes at 70 m.p.h.

NORTH OF SAN FRANCISCO, the freeway extends for some seventy-five miles before suddenly grinding to a halt near Geyserville. There, speeding cars and trucks must slow down as they negotiate the narrow, winding, two-lane road which weaves in and out of some of California's most famous vineyards. From that point on, patches of disconnected freeway appear and disappear as Highway 101 marches on toward the Redwood Wonderland.

At least that's the way it used to be. Now the troublesome stretch of curves near Geyserville is being eliminated. Drivers will no longer have to apply their brakes or inch over to the left to peek around slow-moving trucks. Five, ten, perhaps even fifteen minutes will be saved by the extension of the superhighway.

Few motorists will ever realize it, but they will be driving directly on top of six acres of Frank Nervo's grapes. That's how much the Highway Department took from him to complete their project.

"Did they pay you for it?" I ask.

"No."

"Not even a token?"

"Yeah, a little. But not what it's worth. And they never told us that bank was gonna be there. When we knew, they was already grinding it. There was no reason for it at all." The "bank" is a ten-foot artificial hill supporting four lanes of brand-new concrete roadway. The mound of dirt forms an impenetrable wall between Frank Nervo's house to the west and his winery to the east. It is difficult for my untrained eye to detect why the bank is there: the land is naturally quite flat, and just to the north it even takes a slight drop.

"How come they built it up right here?" I ask.

"The only thing they could say is to cut the grade down for trucks. I said, 'What about the Waldo approach down there?' I've driven it a lotta times. I think it's ten times steeper than this one. The trucks take it or leave it. No, there was something else involved in that bank of dirt. I figure they was just eager to move a lotta dirt and make a big job and spend extra millions of dollars.

"But, hell, that bank throws all the noise of the automobiles right inside the house. Before, the road was level and we didn't get the noise. And they cut off all the vision from the house. We can't see who's down at the winery any more. Before, we could see everything down here, if there was cars down here or . . . Now we can't see nothing. Nothing at *all*. It's up to the top of the roof of the house." To prove his point, Frank ushers me to the door of the small wooden cottage where we've been tasting his wine and raises an arm toward the freeway. There, between the speeding cars and trucks, I catch a glimpse of a rooftop across the way.

"That's your house?"

"That's my house. No, they took too much land. Way too much land. They figured on six lanes for the future. Well, hell, they'd have to bring some more dirt in. If you put two more lanes in, one on each side, then we'll have it right inside the house. The dirt will fall on the house."

"How will you get from your house to the winery when the freeway is completed?" As the crow flies, the house is scarcely one hundred yards from where we stand outside the tasting room. The makeshift crossing which serves him now will soon disappear when the next stretch of road is done.

"Have to go down here a mile, but even so, you got to load it on a trailer. You can't go down the pavement with a tractor."

The problem, it appears, is that not only the house but also some of the vineyards have been isolated from the winery.

"And before, you could just cross right over? You didn't have to load onto a trailer?"

"No, they wasn't able to stop anyone from crossing the pavement then. But I wouldn't want to cross it now anyway because it's risky when the four lanes are open. You know, seventy miles an hour doesn't mean seventy miles an hour. They doing eighty, ninety miles an hour and you wouldn't make it, I tell ya. You wouldn't ever make it across in time. They'd run right over you.

"Another thing, when they first come in here it's just before my crop was ready to harvest. The fellow wanted a bribe. If I gave it to him, he'd wait till I picked my grapes. But I didn't. I offered him a check. He said cash only. He knew if I gave him a check I could turn him in, and that's just what I was gonna do. So they tore up the plants a week before they coulda been picked. He wanted to get back at me for not giving him the bribe.

"Now I want to get this hillside worked out, but I don't know how the hell I'm gonna work it. With the fence in the way I can't get in. So I want to be paid for abandoning the hills. It's a big item for a little vineyard. Those are premium grapes."

"I don't understand. Why do you have to abandon it?"

"Before, we came to the bottom where it's flat. Now there's no flat place to turn around in. Heck, tractors are narrow. They can flop right over. And they got the fence in there. They had to put it in, 'cause they let the deer in. They tore down the old fence when they put in the road. The deer just about killed the vineyard. They was warned about the deer fence, and they didn't listen to me. Then they done the damage, and they put it up quick. I say, well, it's too late now. But I made 'em fence it. But it's not a deer fence—it's half the height of the original one. That one won't even keep a dog out."

"But the main thing now is getting a flat place to maneuver the tractor?"

"It'll flop over. Those tractors are narrow, exceptionally

narrow. About three-foot wide. If you're not an expert you'll flop it over."

"And they never provided for that?"

"Nothing. Never said a word. Well, how can they? They don't understand nothing. They have it just their own way, see? But I made up my mind I'm not gonna keep quiet. Oh, no."

"What'll happen if you don't get in with a tractor?"

"Gotta turn over the land. It'll all dry up pretty soon. We'll get a hell of a fire hazard. Drop a match in there and it'll burn up everything."

"And you have to do it with a tractor?"

"No other way, no other way. We don't know what a horse looks like, whether it's got four legs or two."

"If they don't level it off, what are you going to do?"

"I wanna be paid for it."

"You'll have to abandon it?"

"Yeah."

"All of it? The whole other side there?"

"All of it. Yeah. All but that little piece on top."

"How many acres is that?"

"Well, it's over twelve. And those hills bear heavy. Hill grapes is a premium. No comparison with the flat at all. But it's either abandon it or we'll have to pull out every other row."

"Every other row? How come?"

"Then we might be able to go crossways. Then you could use a bigger tractor, see, wider, so it won't tip over. It'll hug the ground better. But even then I wanna be paid for it. Of course, those wide tractors are cheap—only about twenty-five thousand dollars."

Frank Nervo, a ruddy, country-handsome, middle-aged man who might be older than he looks, has a lot to be angry about. The six acres that lie beneath the freeway are the least of his worries. A ten-foot wall of earth separates his house from his winery, his vineyards from each other. The noise from the traffic is deafening. A hundred-yard walk to work will soon become a two-mile drive, and grapes from across the way will have to be loaded onto a road-worthy trailer to be hauled to the winery. He might have to abandon twelve acres of premium grapes, or else he'll have to buy a wider tractor in order to save half of the grapes. It seems that only the deer have gained an easier access to his vineyard.

When the original Nervos established the winery in 1908, they had no way of foreseeing the present circumstances. Automobiles had only recently been invented; who would have suspected the demands they someday would make? The Nervos situated their operation in the strategic stretch of land between the fledgling roadway and the railroad. Then, it seemed like the wisest thing to do.

But times have changed, and most of Frank's winegrowing neighbors are thinking of selling out. I ask him why. "Well, it's a figure they've never seen before, and they figure they might just as well unload now. The problem, see, is this valley is prime agricultural land, but now they want to take all the agriculture out and put in freeways and developments. Now it's four lanes through our front yard. But it can't stop there. Soon it'll be six, eight, ten lanes, and we won't even have a house left. A highway patrolman came by and told me we shoulda never let them in at all. Once it's there, it'll mean the end of agriculture. The whole county will be developed.

"Over in Napa County they kept the freeway out. If it comes through at all, it'll be on top of the hills, not down in good growing land. But they don't want to put developments up in the hills. It's a problem with septic tanks. You put a coupla houses on a hundred acres and that's all it'll take. The moisture won't go through the sandpan they got up there. It just sits on the surface and soon it's flowing into the neighbor's yard. Down here in the good soil it leaches right on through. So this is where they want to put the developments.

"Still, they could put in sewers up there. That's marginal land. It's not being used for anything else. This here is good growing soil and there's not that much of it left.

"At least now we got a law that you can't divide your land into less than twenties. That should keep the developments out. But how can they tell you what to do with your own land? It's against the First Amendment. I got it right up there on the wall."

"Where?" I ask. I can't quite recall the section of the First Amendment he has in mind. We re-enter the tasting room, and sure enough, a copy of the Bill of Rights is hanging on the wall.

"Right up there. It says you can do anything you want on your own property, as long as it doesn't interfere with your neighbor. You can drill for oil or water or build whatever you want without a permit. If you want to sell it, you got a right to do it. But now they tell you you can't. They make you have a permit for everything. If you put up a building, it's gotta be certified earthquake-proof, they say. But there's not a building in the world that's earthquake-proof. When the quake comes along, *it* decides what to tear down, not some commissioner. They got buildings down in Santa Rosa that are made out of paper, but they say they're up to code. This one out here wasn't built with no permit and it's better than any they got down there."

Frank is angry. His face is tightened behind his dark-rimmed glasses. He is talking nonstop; his voice is loud and clear. He is not trying to sell me wine—he is trying to make me understand. But in a peculiar jump of logic, he has twisted his apparent approval of antisubdivision ordinances into a tirade against all such laws which infringe on individual property rights. How did he manage to change sides so quickly—and so vehemently?

In a way it all makes sense. What he is saying is this: Somebody, something out there, is telling him what's going to happen to him, to his land, to his livelihood. Freeways, developments, laws, permits . . . that's where the power lies.

"I live under so many governments I can't even count them. There's the national, state, county, local, Bay Area, and then all the ordinances and districts. I have to pay taxes to them all, and then they tell me what to do. They tell me I can't burn off my fields because of air pollution. So things just pile up and cause a fire hazard, which is what I got now. The Forestry Department agrees with me. They let me burn for years. But now the Bay Area tells me I can't clean up my own yard. I tell them it's them that's making the smog, not me. I see it coming right up over those hills down by Santa Rosa. It's coming from the refineries down by Richmond. You can smell it, all the chemicals they got in it. It's the gases that are poisonous, not the smoke. But they tell me I can't burn, and I can't tell them nothing. They just keep on doing what they want."

Frank makes few distinctions among the anonymous "they" who have the power to tell others what to do: the Bay Area government, the Richmond oil refineries, the Highway Department, the Earthquake Commissioner. And, of course, there's always the railroad.

"What we have up here is the S.P. [Southern Pacific]. No one likes them. Never have. They own everything. Up by Eureka they own all that land on both sides of the road. Down south, they own the fields and are growing grapes. Now they own the trucks. They're behind these new freeways. Why pay money to fix up their own tracks when they can get the government to build roads for them? I'm trying to boycott them, but it's hard, 'cause you don't know who they are. 'Just tell me your names,' I tell them. I'll boycott them all. They're all one company."

"What did they do to you?"

"Well, they get ornery. We just had the new ties put in on our spur out here, spent a thousand dollars to get the ties put it. Two years after, they yank it out. After we put all that money out. They're dirty, boy."

"*You* spent the money?"

"Oh, yeah. Any repair we're responsible for. They'll do the work, but they'll bill you for it. And I ran 'em off. I caught 'em several times. I ran 'em off the job and they had to come in the long way, down the track. And they were just that dirty."

"Why did they want to take it out?"

"I don't know. There's someone wanted to get that spur out. I can't figure who it was. Anyway, it's gone."

"Before they took the spur out, did you deal a lot with the railroad?"

"Gallo went by truck. We deal mostly with them. I guess Gallo was in back of it. He wants to ship by truck, not by rail. And if you don't move a certain amount of freight per year, or don't use it at all, they'll pull it out from under you. Other wineries, too. You have to use it, or they'll pull it out."

"So that's why they pulled it out, because you weren't using it?"

"Yeah, but by golly, even so . . . Anyway, the spur's taken out. All we got is the ties left. If you put the ties in, they're your ties. But they take the rails out. They say the rails belong to them. I say, for the price we pay to put the ties in, the whole thing belongs to me. But they don't listen. After all, it's on their property. As far as that goes, you'd have a hell of a time in court. It's not worthwhile. They're too big to fight anyway."

"What about the highway? Are you filing a suit on them?"

"We're gonna try to settle out of court. Say, wanna taste another little wine you never tasted before?"

"What's that?"

"Or I don't think you have. They call it a Malvoisie. This is a new lot, but it won't hold up on the shelf. Drops its sediment, 'cause it's taken out of the tank without no clarification." Frank pours me out a paper cup of Malvoisie, then points back over his shoulder to the Zinfandel. "Now those over there, those are finished wines. They'll hold up in the restaurants or anywheres. But, see, we're only hand-bottlers. That's quite a job to hand-bottle. It's just a sideline to us. We do bulk mostly, just ship right out to Gallo or any of the big wineries. But we had the hand-bottling since 1935, so we got a lot of people scattered around. Our trouble is we can't fill the orders. We got so many orders standing here, we don't pay attention to the distributors coming in. Had one here early today wanted to handle our wine. But if you want to go distribute out of state, you have to be set for it. Leo, he's pretty well modernized about it. We're not. We're hand-bottlers. I think we're about the only ones that hand-bottle—and it's a *hell* of a slow job. To do a big job, you have to have a machine, 'cause everything has to be just right."

"Would you mind if I wrote it all down?" I ask while sipping my paper-cup wine.

"You mean on the highway?"

"Yeah, just what you told me."

"Hell, criticize it as high as you want. They've done a terrific amount of damage. In fact, I'm waiting for the chief to come up here now and have it out. We don't figure this settled yet. But it's a long wait. I'm tired of waiting. They're hard to move. I know they don't want to be bothered, but they'll have to come over. This is election year for all of them, but that doesn't bother them, 'cause they don't depend on the farmers' vote." I don't quite understand who "them" refers to. The "chief"? Who's that? Since when do the folks at the Highway Department have to stand for election? Again, Frank makes few distinctions among the anonymous "they," the people in power.

"How are you going to get a settlement if it's not in court?"

"There's another group. I think the unions use it a lot. They use an Arbitrary Board, I think. I think there's about five men involved in that board. You get a more sensible group that way. They operate on a fee. It's established, it's not a fly-by-night. I forget what they call it. I got the papers up at the house. It's highly established.

"But I'm positive I'm gonna get quite a bit of money from them, 'cause there was no public hearings. They were held behind closed doors, and there's a law that reads there has to be public hearings. There wasn't a single public hearing. There wasn't any at all that we know of, and we got the records of all of them. The thing was all done behind closed doors. And you know where the acceptance . . ."

"The what?"

"In the city of Los Angeles. The route was adopted in the city of Los Angeles. When we found out, my brother went down with a plane, the meeting was over."

"Not in Sacramento?"

"No, sir. Los Angeles. Supposed to been held not in Los Angeles, but here locally. It was held in Los Angeles purposely, so we wouldn't get there in time. Because they knew there'd be a terrific objection. They didn't want no objection, see? We got wind of it. . . ."

"Did they publish notices about it, or how did you . . .?"

"No, I don't know how we found out. I think someone found out through the office in San Francisco. But that wasn't the bid for the highway. That's the plans, way back when the first plans were originally adopted. They adopted the plans in Los Angeles County."

"When was that, about ten years ago?"

"Maybe not. Pretty near a good eight. If I woulda had the right groups on my side . . ."

"What are the 'right groups'?"

"I coulda got the Sierra, and I coulda got the Environmental Club, and this road woulda never been here. It woulda been back up in the hills where it belongs. Freeways have been stopped all over the place. The Sierra Club down in San Francisco, they stop them all the time. It's getting so they can tell them where to put the freeways and where not to."

"Did you try to get the Sierra Club to help you out?"

"They sent someone down. He said he was the head of it, but I could tell by the way he talked he was just a secretary. He didn't know anything. I told him I'd talk to the president." The Sierra Club, in Frank's mind, is included in the "they" that have the power, the ones who decide where freeways will (or won't) be built. He doesn't know precisely who it is, but *somebody* must decide those things. There's only one thing Frank knows for sure: it's not *him* that's calling the shots.

"Did you ever try to get any organized opposition to the freeway?"

"You don't get no support from nobody anyway on anything you do. Their word doesn't mean nothing. Their signature don't mean nothing. You can sign a petition, but they don't mean it. We went through that before. You talk to them, they tell you one thing, then if they got the advantage they'll double-cross you and go just the opposite. That's been proven on lots of things—way, way back."

So Frank Nervo stands alone, straddling the monster that has bisected his land. He feels isolated from his would-be allies, just as his house has been isolated from his winery. He would like to be more, but, alas, he is at best a small thorn in the impenetrable sides of the lifeless creature that has come to dominate his life. "No, it's all wrong. Wrong as can be. And the worst is they haven't paid for it. They haven't paid for the damages."

Can he make them pay? He hopes so, but, ultimately, there's

not a hell of a lot Frank has to say in the matter, just as there wasn't a hell of a lot he could do about the freeway coming through in the first place. And that's what makes him mad: that the power is out of his hands. "Sure, I'll fight it. But it's there to stay for now. For a long time to come."

13

Congestion in the Redwoods

Soon after you enter Humboldt County from the south on Highway 101, you drive into a cool, dark, verdant forest of towering redwood trees. This is Richardson Grove, one of California's 22 coast redwood parks, named in honor of the state's 25th governor.

The park's tranquil setting is one of shadows and semi-darkness. Even when the sun is at its zenith, only a fraction of the light filters through the closely growing trees and their protective branches. Sounds are shut out by the profusion of plant life, and the wind is tempered by the tall trees. The forest stillness is not easily forgotten.

So READS the official brochure, but this is not how I experience Richardson Grove State Park. What I noticed first and remember most is the traffic. The highway passes right through the towering trees, filling the clear country air with exhaust and an incessant motorized hum. The automotive drone is punctuated only by the acceleration and deceleration of logging and lumber trucks, which blow their horns to give warning to the pedestrians who crowd the side of the road. The traffic grinds to a halt as cars, campers, and trailers form a waiting line for the limited space in the overcrowded parking lot in the shade of the redwoods. Once safely parked, the cars, weighted down with luggage on their roofs, spew forth men, women, and children, almost all of whom bear cameras around their necks. Awaiting the tourists on either side of the highway are fenced walkways through the trees, but between the paths there is a conspicuous lack of undergrowth, for much of the "profusion of plant life" has long since been trampled or otherwise destroyed. Numerous wooden signs, tastefully done and strategically placed, explain the park rules. A fallen log is barricaded, with a warning to adventuresome children: "Hazardous—Keep Off." Familiar red fire hydrants appear here and there. Electric lights hang from the trees, with their bulbs softened by wooden shades and their wiring half concealed in the grooves of the bark. Telephone poles, dwarfed by the gigantic redwoods, carry more wires overhead.

The main attraction and center of activity is Camp Richardson Lodge, a long wooden building shared by a post office, grocery store, dining room, and gift shop. Inside the gift shop, a young boy is playing with toy logging trucks on the shiny linoleum floor. "If you break something in here, I'm going to break you," says Uncle Paul, a decidedly overweight man with a falsetto voice and receding black hair who is sporting a blue and white checked shirt which hangs out over his pants. The child keeps playing.

"Can I buy this?" the kid finally asks his patron.

"What's the price on it?" The child is too young to understand about price tags. Uncle Paul takes a look.

"That's too much. I can't afford it."

The boy disappears, but soon he is back with a still bigger truck. "Can I buy this one?"

"That's twice as big, it costs twice as much."

The boy might be young, but he is no dope. Uncle Paul has backed himself into a corner. "Then can I buy this one? It's small. Can I get the small one?"

Minutes later, three small logging trucks appear on the checkout stand as Uncle Paul fills out a twenty-dollar traveler's check.

Each summer tens of thousands of enthusiastic visitors like Uncle Paul and his nephew move directly from their cars to the gift shop, scarcely bothering to glance at the trees overhead. Once inside, they are presented with an awesome array of redwood artifacts: treasure chests, tic-tac-toe boards, penny banks, salt and pepper shakers, pen and pencil holders. One whole corner is devoted to clever sayings ("Think—and surprise us all") inscribed on redwood plaques. Clocks, lamps, and thermometers are mounted in redwood burls. One large redwood slab, selling for sixty dollars, has been carved into the shape of a knight in shining armor and painted silver and red. A foot-long burl with plastic flowers growing out of it goes for fifty dollars. Two small cubes of polished myrtlewood, labeled "bookends" for those who cannot figure it out by themselves, cost fifteen dollars. And for the less wealthy customers, there are plastic squirrels that climb the walls and shellacked pine cones joined together in the shape of owls. The idea of it all, of course, is for the tourists to claim a piece of the Redwood Wonderland for their very own. Only the sunglasses, it seems, are of practical use to the travelers.

Across the highway from the Lodge is an educational display where the story of the redwoods is told in graphic detail by signs and visual examples. Here one learns how to discover floods and fires of the past by reading the trunks of the trees. Some of it is interesting, some seems overly simplistic. (*"Animals of the Redwoods*. From the stately black-tailed deer to the frisky squirrels and chipmunks and even the tiny salamanders, all have a place in the natural harmony of life in the redwood forest region.") Despite pleas to the contrary, initials and other hieroglyphics are inscribed on much of the display material.

Above the educational exhibit is the campground, hidden from the highway by sight but not by sound or smell. The pace is slower here than down below. Some of the folks are playing cards, chess, and badminton and riding bikes, while others are reading or listening to the ball game. Someone is sweeping the ground. Each campsite is equipped with a standardized set of gear: tents, ice chests, stoves, lanterns, lounge chairs. Charcoal and Presto logs are set out beside the fireplaces, for there are no dead branches along the ground. ("Gathering of firewood prohibited," read the signs.) For those who have come ill prepared, a sack of mill ends can be purchased for a dollar. These mill ends, it turns out, are given to the park in lieu of rent by a mill that is on state land.

The campground is a re-creation of suburban life, but with one important difference: life goes on in the open, not behind closed doors. People talk with each other for no reason at all. Laundry hangs to dry where everyone can see it. Smells of spaghetti and hamburger fill the air. But the cars and campers and trailers still dominate the space—and people's minds as well. I pass by a young, healthy-looking woman as she tells her child she is going to the store for some milk. She then gets in her car, which surprises me since she is less than a hundred yards from her destination by a pleasant foot trail. Because of the intricacies of campground roadways, on the other hand, she is at least a half mile away by road. She has trouble starting her car, but finally succeeds. I walk leisurely down to the store and I wait around for five or ten minutes. She finally arrives, purchases a quart of milk, and departs.

Past the campground are the hiking trails. "Lookout Point," according to the sign, is only three tenths of a mile away. I walk the trail and see not a soul, a sudden contrast from the congestion below. When I arrive at Lookout Point, what I find is a panoramic view of the highway as it emerges from the south end of the park.

Guided tours along the trails are given once a day, with each day's hike leading to a different place. Some are hard, three-mile treks; others are less strenuous:

FRIDAY 9/10 MI. 2 HRS.	*River Trail* . . . Ranger Keith Williams leads this short gentle walk that ends at the Coffee Center for coffee and "Smokey Bear" Kool-Aid.

The high point of the park's activities is the evening campfire. The "campfire center" in Richardson Grove, however, is not really a fire but a stage—the fire pit itself has been relegated to the side wings. It is Friday evening, and some two hundred people have gathered for the eight-thirty program. There are no blacks, two Oriental youths, and the rest are all white. Children fill the first two rows, couples and families are in the middle, while a handful of adolescents stand in the back and off to the sides. They are, by and large, hardy-looking folks: the men

187

wear hunting caps and sport week-old beards; the women wear parkas and are not afraid to show their graying hair. The kids, I suspect, are being raised to enjoy outdoor life.

A young mustachioed ranger takes the microphone. "We're going to play 'Rip the Ranger' for a while before we start the show, so go ahead and raise your hands."

"Why can't you publish a program each night?" asks a middle-aged woman.

"When was a bear last sighted around here?" asks a heavyset man.

"How cold will it get tonight?" asks a ten-year-old boy.

The answers are short and to the point. Suddenly another mustachioed ranger takes hold of the microphone. "Hi! How many people know me? Raise your hands." Some hands are raised. "How many people don't know me?" Other hands are raised. "Okay, how many people didn't raise their hands either time?" A few more hands go up. Here, I say to myself, is a master M.C.—he leaves no loopholes to stay uninvolved. "Well, you have to either know me or not. My name is Keith Williams. But I don't know you. So on the count of three, everyone yell out your name." He counts, and everybody yells at once.

The questions continue: "Last night we were on a walk and we got attacked by something. . . ."

"Probably a park attendant," Keith Williams interrupts.

"We thought maybe it was a bat. Do you have bats around here?"

"Yeah, we have some bats. But they really don't attack people, they just come out at twilight and fly around. But a park attendant, now that's another . . ."

"Hey!" a young boy yells. "There's two deer down there by the river."

Keith Williams goes over to the side of the stage and looks. Everyone else stays where he is. "He's right," Keith says. "There's two deer down there. Everybody go look if you want." With permission granted, a hundred people leave their seats to look at the deer. When things settle back down a few minutes later, the ranger explains why people shouldn't feed the deer and tame them, only to make them easy prey for future hunters.

"Well, we have a campfire tonight," Keith continues. "So I guess we'll have to light it. How will we decide who gets to light it?"

"Maybe someone has a birthday today," the other ranger observes.

"That's it. Who has a birthday today?"

"I have one tomorrow!" screams a girl who can hardly contain herself. Her raised hand is shaking from the excitement.

"Can anyone beat that?"

"I have one today," says a boy toward the back. "July twentieth." He gets to light the fire, with the help of the other ranger.

"While he's lighting the fire," says Keith, "let's let everyone know there's a campfire tonight." On the count of three, everyone yells "Campfire!" We hear the echo from across the river. Another yell, another echo. The place, as they say, is hopping. And *everybody* yells, not just the kids.

"We have a rule around here that everybody does what I tell them to do. Within reason, of course. All right, everybody raise their hand."

Most everyone does.

"If you see someone who isn't raising their hand, point to them." The deviants are thus revealed.

"All right, who wants to sing?"

A few reluctant hands go up.

"Well, we'll have everyone singing before the night is out. We have a bat named Herman who comes down and flies in the hair of everyone who doesn't sing. We're going to start by singing 'Home . . . on . . . the . . . Range.' Does everybody know it?"

We sing the song, swaying from side to side with the gesture of Keith Williams's hand. Everyone joins in. The adults have slightly embarrassed grins on their faces, but they are clearly enjoying themselves nonetheless.

Ranger Williams notices a boy in the back who's not singing.

The ranger leaves the stage, grabs the boy, and carries him up front to the microphone. The boy finally joins in with the rest.

The words to "Old MacDonald Had a Farm" flash on the screen. Again, everybody sings happily.

Finally, the main attraction commences: a quiz game known as "Redwood Bowl," which is patterned after TV's "College Bowl." The questions are true/false, multiple choice, and the like. For the people who have read the park's educational display, the answers come easily: size of the tallest tree, which species of tree is the oldest ever found, etc. Worked in and around each question are informative slides. A marvelous performance indeed: a slide show with no one bored! Not a soul leaves the theater until the projector breaks down midway.

The success of Keith Williams's showmanship is the success of the park: it serves its visitors well, it gives them what they want. They get to see, to live in, and to learn about the redwoods with little effort of their own and in a nonthreatening environment. The trees, as it were, have been tamed: they have been placed behind fences like caged animals in the zoo, with their native habitat appropriately altered to accommodate the tourists who have come to gaze upon them. The ancient redwoods are thus transformed into a twentieth-century commodity. They exist to be consumed by human beings, to be fenced and photographed and exploited in a thousand different ways. Privately owned groves are made into the Singing Trees Resort, Confusion Hill Mystery, Living Chimney Tree—as if just being a majestic redwood forest were not enough!

Richardson Grove is no isolated phenomenon. Tourism is now the second-largest industry in Humboldt County—the first, of course, is logging. From an environmental point of view, tourism would seem to be preferable to logging: once a tree has been cut and made into lumber, that's the end of it for quite some time; with the land devoted to tourism, however, every year the tourists can come back to look at the same old trees. Have not the state parks, after all, managed to preserve at least a token of the virgin redwood forests? Tourism, in a sense, is an indefinitely renewable resource. And tourism, unlike logging, tends to remain centered in accessible locations along the highway, thus leaving the rest of the countryside relatively untouched.

But what are the effects of tourism on the local folk, the people along the Edges of backcountry life? Do their lives remain unchanged, or are they, like the redwoods, somehow "tamed"?

There are serious sociological consequences for a community that embraces a tourist economy as a way of life. Tourism inevitably focuses on service to outsiders, and it necessitates an adjustment to the cultural values of the people being served. When the local person who is running the motel or restaurant projects the notion of what he thinks the tourist wants, he naturally gravitates to the standardized conception of American culture. There's very rarely any attempt to make a local art or a local menu; from the architecture of the motels to the nature of the meals at the restaurants, the support institutions which accompany tourism tend to be the same wherever we go. The proprietor must reach the tourist at a level he's familiar with, for tourists don't want their expectations upset. The notion of comfort is paramount. When tourists come into an area, they tend to surround themselves with things they already know: they bring in their camper trucks and their deck chairs from patios back home. What that really means is they're not prepared for what used to be called adventure; they're prepared to function pretty much as normal. But since the tourists are generally on vacation, they do like to travel under conditions in which somebody else cooks, somebody else makes the beds, somebody else does the work that enables life to continue. It is the local people, therefore, that are turned into the maids. An economy of service is thus easily transformed into an economy of subservience.

On a purely economic level, the transformation of land into recreational uses can drive the people of the Edges from their homes. Their land takes on an inflated value, and their taxes consequently burgeon. Since taxes for landed folk account for a major portion of their yearly expenditures, they might easily be forced to sell out—or at least to sell off some of their ranch. The land, in effect, falls into the laps of the only kind of people who can afford to buy it in this day and age: first the real estate investors and speculators, then the middle- and upper-middle-class urbanites who use it on an occasional, transient basis.

Finally, there is the question of how the land itself is being treated. The local folk might graze it and log it—sometimes with harmful effects—but simply because the land is *theirs* they are more likely to treat it with a modicum of respect. The recreationists, however, the summer Sunday folks, have less at stake in the land they visit. "Some days you see twenty-five or thirty dune buggies out there," says Paul Smith, a Honeydew rancher. "Those people are up the creeks, in our cabins. They are everywhere. They kill our sheep, run up through the grass, and spin wheelies and throw their beer cans around."

Other old-timers echo these sentiments. "They put roads in here for the tourists, civilization comes right along," says Frank, the old Wobbly from Whitethorn. "But this ain't civilization, this is the backhills. People come in—like ants, like bees. Be so many people, you can't get your net in the water. Then there be no fish, no nothing. I know, I seen it happen down the way. And I know why they do it, too—money. Is there anything else? They do it all just for money. They're sick in the head—educated sick."

Paul Smith, Frank, and others just like them—they are the ones with the most to lose. Some are ranchers, some ex-loggers, but they all have ties with the land. They tend gardens, raise chickens, hunt deer, chop wood, can their food, build their own shelter—the everyday tasks that keep life on its proper path. They share a world which is small and intimate, a world on a human scale. And the young folks, too, the ones who have adopted these agrarian ways—these are the people whose lives, whose culture, are being threatened as tourism reaches outward into the Edges of the backcountry.

Tourism, in short, tends to make our towns into auto rows, our people into paid employees of the summer travelers. We are slowly but surely becoming tied to the conception that the rest of the world has of us: we are drive-through trees, curio shops, state parks; we exist to provide food, gas, lodging, and amusement for our sightseeing visitors. With an increasing proportion of local people directly dependent on the tourist trade, and with the tourists themselves consisting almost exclusively of white, middle-class Americans, we find that for our very survival we must adopt a standardized set of codes and values. We must, after all, give the folks what they want. The crude, rough-and-tumble backcountry ethic has thus all but disappeared in the face of polite service.

Whatever happened to that old saying "When in Rome, do as the Romans do"? Somehow, somewhere along the line, it has been subtly altered: "When in Rome, have the Romans do it for you."

14

Damning the Dams

WHITETHORN, to me, is town. It is there that I receive my mail, and I shop at its general store. When my kids are old enough to go to school, that is where they will go. I was understandably concerned, therefore, by the rumors to the effect that a dam might soon be built which would turn much of Whitethorn Valley into a lake.

Rumors will be rumors, yet one day a small sign appeared on the post-office wall: a public meeting was to be held at the cafe in Honeydew by the Department of Water Resources concerning the dam they proposed to build on the Mattole River near Whitethorn. The meeting place was a four-hour round-trip drive from my home; nevertheless, I was determined to go to find out what the whole thing was about.

We pulled into the Old Mattole Cafe just at the appointed time, yet a meeting was nowhere in sight. Indeed, there were only three booths and a half dozen stools at the counter—hardly enough space for a public hearing. We soon discovered it was the *New* Mattole Cafe we were after, a mile or two down the road. But we paused for a bowl of homemade soup and a piece of homemade pie.

"They're gonna put a dam up in here?" asked the hefty woman who was serving up the food.

"They're always talking about it," responded a wiry, weathered man who was feasting on the daily special in one of the booths. "But I'll believe it when I see it."

"They'll ruin the whole darn thing," said the hardy hostess. "There's only two rivers left that're clear, this and the Smith. Right after the rains, they clear right up. But they're the only ones left." Indeed, "Mattole" is an Indian name meaning "clear water." No one knows exactly why, but the Mattole just doesn't get as murky as the rest of the rivers around.

"Well," said the man in the booth, assuming a philosophical tone, "long about the end of fall, all the fishermen we get in here just about dam the thing up anyways."

Over at the New Mattole Cafe, the meeting was already in progress. Ed Barnes, dressed casually in a sports shirt but still standing out from the crowd (about fifty people) clad mostly in working clothes, was using maps and charts to explain what the Department of Water Resources had in mind. There were two possible sites for the dam, one just above the town of White-thorn and one a few miles below it. The colored area on the first map showed the Redwoods Monastery, a virgin stand of timber, and several small homesteads all under water; a large stretch of level ranching land and a score of houses were inundated by the second.

The reason for it all was simple: the "Fish Enhancement Project," as it was called, might add forty-five days a year of fishing time to the lower Mattole River by regulating the flow of water. "As I'm sure you all know," said Ed Barnes, "the salmon and steelhead populations have been declining in recent years. If we can manage to increase the flow of water in the late summer and early fall, the fish could get up the river sooner." He then cited the amount of water he thought would be needed, and the amount the proposed dam could supply. He assured his audience that the dam was a modest one: it would only take twelve million dollars to construct, and would be used solely for the purpose of fish enhancement. There would be no electric generators, nor would the water be rerouted toward Los Angeles.

The proposal was an interesting one. How could anti-dam conservationists attack a fish enhancement project? Aren't they the ones who have been complaining the loudest about the rapid depopulation of salmon and steelhead? Dams, often assailed as being one of the major causes of the problem, were now being offered as a possible solution.

But the conservationists were not about to jump on the dam-building bandwagon. Philip Starr, speaking for the newly formed Mattole Soil and Water Conservation Committee, observed that each fish caught for the next generation would cost the taxpayers about two hundred dollars. He pointed out that by Ed Barnes's own calculations the sun-drenched water released from the lake might be hot enough to kill the fish which were allegedly being helped. He bemoaned the displacement of people, the inundation of virgin redwoods. He painted a vivid picture of the concrete monster which would come to dominate the lives of the people who lived beneath it, and proposed in its stead that the watershed itself be improved by more natural means.

The arguments were only what one might expect. Ed Barnes had heard the environmentalists before, and he was not about to change his mind because they opposed his dam.

Robert McKee, a local contractor-developer whose grandfather's homestead would be flooded by one of the dam sites, then offered another alternative: to build several smaller holding ponds way up on the tributaries, where no one would be displaced. Ed Barnes listened, but again he was unconvinced. The brainstorming of a layman, he felt, was no match for the professional competence of a trained engineer. The smaller dams, he assured McKee, would simply never work.

But if professionalism was his fare, Barnes was soon to be outdone. Sheldon Wolin, a professor of politics at Princeton University, whose summer home was but a mile from one of the proposed lakes, predicted (and Barnes would be the first to agree) that with the lake would come the tourists. Directing his attention to tourism and speaking in a melodious, well-cultured voice, Wolin analyzed the possible results:

It seems to me that there are three considerations that are very important in gauging the effect of committing a community to tourism. One is, I think, the obvious fact that it is a very fly-by-night and fragile economy, that it brings in money relatively quickly, but it doesn't generate any real structure to the economy at all. The second consideration is the skyrocketing of land values that occurs, and the consequent rise in tax structure, all of which make it very difficult for country-oriented people to make any kind of stab at owning land. The third aspect of tourism (and in some ways it seems to me the most fundamental even though it is the least tangible) is that the kind of ethos that surrounds it, the set of relationships and the atmosphere that it develops, are an atmosphere of service to strangers, to people who come in to spend the night in your motel or eat at your restaurant or take gas from your gas station. You don't see them again; they come, they go; the whole relationship is fugitive and ephemeral. And I think there is inevitably a subservience built into it that isn't there when people who serve each other know each other, whose faces are familiar, who see each other day in and day out. When tourism becomes, so to speak, the defining feature of the profile of a community, there is a dependence on pleasing those who really mean nothing to you, whose relationships are remote and abstract and very dehumanizing.

It was an awesome performance indeed, perhaps unparalleled in the history of the New Mattole Cafe. Still, it was possible to dismiss such arguments as the too subtle workings of the intellectuals' imagination. Intellectuals, after all, like environmentalists, are familiar foes to the proponents of dams.

Next came the nuns, the sisters from the Redwoods Monastery, which was in danger of being submerged. Their statement was short and to the point: "We try not to hurt a soul," said one of the sisters. "We only wish to be left in peace. I don't understand that we must move. Why? Just for fish? Please, let us stay. We plead for your mercy."

At last, here was testimony that Ed Barnes found impossible to ignore. It is a difficult matter, politically speaking, to spit in the face of religion, to invoke the wrath of God. "We have just heard the strongest argument of the evening," he admitted. Still, he tried to minimize the effect of his losses: "Of course, no one ever wants to be moved out," he said in a fatalistic tone, as if to suggest that the nuns' plea for mercy, while emotionally appealing, was somehow lacking in objectivity. "But whenever a dam or a road is proposed, a few people *have* to be moved. That's just the way it is."

The evening was progressing badly for poor Ed Barnes. So far, not a soul had come to his support: a conservationist, a local developer, an intellectual, and the nuns had all opposed his dam. Yet the downriver ranchers had not yet spoken, and he had hopes they might come to his aid. Why else, after all, had he scheduled the meeting down here in Honeydew, separated by thirty miles of half-paved, winding mountain roads from the proposed sites of the dam and the major population center of the area? The nuns had offered their chapel, but how can you realistically hold a hearing on a dam in the middle of a virgin redwood grove which the dam was about to destroy? No, it made more sense to speak to the downriver folks, the ones who might receive the benefit from all those extra fish.

But it just didn't happen that way. "We don't want any more fish," said Mrs. Etter, a vociferous rancher from Honeydew. "When there's fish there's fishermen, and then all we get is headaches. Whenever there's a fish run, everyone in the state seems to know it in about fifteen minutes, 'cause they're all down here lined up on the river so thick that we can't even get our own poles in." And the rest of the ranchers agreed. "I don't *want* my land values to go up," said another old-timer. "All I get then is higher taxes."

The ranchers' attitude, in the context of modern American society, was highly unorthodox. It was not what Ed Barnes expected. Here he was offering them a deeper river during the summer drought, with the possibility of increased revenues from the tourist trade. The land-rich but money-poor ranchers would have little difficulty in selling off some second-home parcels for nice high prices—and yet they wanted none of it. Like the nuns, all the ranchers seemed to want was to be left alone. Ranching, for them, was a way of life. The ones who wanted higher times had already left for the cities and towns.

So Ed Barnes, in the end, had to stand by himself. Save for the co-worker who came with him, he was the only one in the room who did not oppose the project. I began to feel for the man: here he had spent a year of his life studying the prospects for a dam, and now, in one night, the whole darn thing was quickly fading from his grasp. He began to soften his tone.

"Well," he said as the meeting neared its end, "I guess the people have spoken. If no one wants it . . ."

But would this be the end of the Whitethorn Dam? What did that meeting really mean? His report had already been pre-pared; it had cost $100,000 to complete. It was due to be sub-mitted two weeks hence, and it would probably still go through —perhaps with a warning that strong opposition from the local population could certainly be expected. Sheldon Wolin, appre-hensive of the limited impact of public hearings, wanted more of a say than that: "What we would like to see, instead of the usual kind of bureaucratic policy which is laid down after a study is made and the public is duly consulted and mystified by the study, is some kind of really innovative arrangement between local people and the government agencies, in which we would be brought in as participants rather than just as passive people who are likely to stand up on their hind legs and object, or simply acquiesce." But no such "innovative arrangement" was devel-oped that night.

Nevertheless, most everybody was pretty happy with the outcome of the meeting. Had not Ed Barnes modified his stance by the end? Personally, I was not so sure. We struck up a con-versation outside the door once the rest of the folks had left.

"I believe a dam is the answer," Ed said. "But I need a place to prove my point. I just don't understand why you people don't want it. What do you think of Clear Lake and Tahoe?" His enthusiastic tone indicated that he thought I most certainly would be in approval.

"I think they're polluted," I said.

"Wouldn't you like to live near a big lake?"

"No, I wouldn't."

"It'd be beautiful."

"But there'd be a lot of motorboats and . . ."

"Yeah, I know. Hundreds, maybe thousands." His eyes lit up. "I live under Shasta, and I love it."

Now, after the meeting was over, we were coming to the heart of the matter. The fish downstream were almost irrelevant as far as Ed Barnes was concerned: it was the lake that really counted. A lover of boats and boating, Ed wanted to be involved in building a lake of his own, but he was having trouble finding a spot to put it. "Everywhere I go," he pleaded, "I run into people like you. Don't you realize that if the lake went in, you could sell out for a fortune and move somewhere else?"

Try as he might, Ed Barnes could not grasp that this was our *home*, that above all else we wanted to stay where we were. The American experience of mobility had permeated his being. I tried to explain about the community he had just encountered: we are country folk, young and old, who feel we have ties with the land. We build our own houses, till our own soil, raise our own stock—and we do not wish to be pushed aside by a dam.

"Of course nobody wants to be moved out," he repeated, once again dismissing our position as emotionally biased. "But sometimes it just has to be done."

The Mad River empties into the Pacific Ocean fifty miles north of the Mattole. At the same time the Department of Water Resources offered to dam up the Mattole in order to help the salmon and steelhead trout, other governmental agencies were seeking to build a dam on the Mad—a dam that would kill off 10,500 of those very same species. Some of the oceangoing fish would be isolated behind the dam, while others would be trapped in front of it, cut off from thirty-five miles of potential spawning beds upstream. The gravel spawning beds beneath the dam, meanwhile, would be covered with silt. The downstream fish would also have to suffer higher water temperatures and increased turbidity—both of which can be lethal to salmon and steelhead trout.

Butler Valley Dam, if constructed, would have been 320 feet high and would have turned nine miles of the Mad River into a 2,360-acre lake. It was a multipurpose project: water resources, flood control, and recreation. The Army Corps of Engineers would build it, and it was to be financed jointly by the federal government and Humboldt County, but the county could take a hundred years to pay its share. Before Butler Valley Dam could become a reality, however, Humboldt County had to agree to the contract. The Board of Supervisors found themselves split down the middle on the controversial project and consequently decided to put the matter to a popular vote. The vote would not be legally binding, but it was sure to have its effect.

Outlying districts such as my own were excluded from the special election, but word of the debate got around. Immediately after the hearing on the Whitethorn Dam, I headed north to the county seat to see what all the commotion was about. The town, I found, was hopping. As I drove toward Eureka, I happened to tune in my radio to a heated public debate. Later that night, the plastic-coated booths of Denny's Coffee Shop (not often a political hot spot) were filled with talk on Butler Valley.

Everybody was taking sides. Advocates of the dam included union leaders, who hoped that some of the construction jobs would fall their way, and local businessmen, who hoped to stimulate the economy. Also supporting the dam were a group of land speculators who had bought up large tracts of adjacent property for purposes of subdivision should Butler Valley indeed be turned into a lake. Opponents included small property owners, students, environmentalists, sport and commercial fishermen, and Indians—each for their own separate reasons.

The differences in political style were classic. The office of the Y.E.S. Committee (Your Economic Survival) was situated in the heart of downtown Eureka and staffed with middle-aged women, party faithfuls fulfilling their civic obligations. There was a lot of money to spend on mass-media advertisements, but not a whole lot of manpower for grass-roots work. The Concerned Citizens' Campaign Committee, by contrast, centered their anti-dam activity in a warehouse in the redevelopment area, with a bulldozer pounding away at the sidewalk not five feet from the main desk. Depending exclusively on small contributions, the anti-dam folks spent most of their time and energy in a door-to-door campaign, distributing flyers and talking to the people.

As its name suggests, the Y.E.S. Committee focused primarily on the issue of economic growth. "Don't let the opponents confuse you with half truths and untruths," warned Helge Paulson, a former county assessor. "The only *real* issue is whether we prosper with moderate growth or stagnate with a no-growth economy." Humboldt county, with twice the national unemployment rate, had experienced a 5 percent decline in population during the 1960's as the logging industry began to run out of trees to harvest. Butler Valley Dam was thus seen as a cure-all for the county's economic ills: it would serve as a "psychological symbol" of growth, according to the Economic Impact Statement of the Corps of Engineers. "People here are looking for something—anything—to grab on to that will bring development," said one of the county supervisors.

Yet in these days of environmental awareness, the advocates of dams and other human manipulations of the natural landscape have come to speak the language of ecology as well as economics. ("I've probably been an environmentalist longer than anyone else here," said dam builder Ed Barnes at the Honeydew meeting.) The consulting firm of Winzler and Kelley, in their official report to the county which spoke strongly in favor of the Butler Valley project, recommended the creation of "environmental water which will have the sole purpose of accommodating the recreationist on rivers of the North Coast." How does a man-made lake surrounded by fifty vertical feet of lifeless, baked earth become known as "environmental water"? How can a man who wishes to substitute fertile valleys and virgin redwoods with a lake full of motorboats consider himself an "environmentalist"? The word has obviously become a political tool which can be used rather loosely to support any and every position.

And yet, ironically, the opponents of Butler Valley Dam scrupulously avoided overemphasizing the environmental issues. Fearful of coming on as naïve conservationists, they went straight to the voters' hearts with bread-and-butter arguments. To call oneself a "no-growth ecologist" in an economically depressed area would have been political suicide; "no-growth" had become a dirty word, just as "communism" was considered taboo in the Cold War era. "Now, I'm not one of those no-growth nuts who place squirrels and rabbits over people," an anti-dam spokesman said at a public debate. "I want to see our community prosper just as much as the next guy." The opponents thus focused their energies on showing how the dam would be a failure even on its own economic terms: the construction jobs would be seasonal and temporary, the securing of the flood plains for commercial development could only be accomplished by the elimination of productive farmland, and the lake itself would be too muddy for both swimmers and fish. "The prognosis for the reservoir fishery is not good," said the Environmental Impact Statement of the Corps of Engineers. "However, it will have the capability of providing many mandays of fishing time." People, in other words, would be welcome to come to "Blue Lake" to fish—just so long as they were prepared not to catch very many.

It was, in its way, a mud-slinging campaign. There were charges and countercharges, and a high-level campaign official decided to resign when the fighting got too dirty. The local newspaper, the *Times-Standard*, became embroiled in the controversy when managing editor Dan Walters was relieved of his duties. The problem lay not so much in Walters's politics (both he and the publisher were strong advocates of the dam) as in his professional policies: he believed in keeping his own feelings limited to the editorial page, while giving full play to both sides of the raging debate elsewhere in the paper. But some of the *Times-Standard*'s biggest advertisers, also pro-dam, took issue with this policy: "We think you should either be for us or against us," they said. So Walters was removed.

Times-Standard reporter Richard Harris, after writing about the Walters incident for an independent magazine, was likewise let go. Publisher Jerry Colby felt he had to fire Harris because "the young man insinuated . . . that the newspaper, his employer, would not report the news in an objective manner."

The paper itself had thus become an issue. Dam opponents felt the news coverage quickly became one-sided: the opening of the anti-dam committee appeared at the bottom of the obituary page, while the launching of the pro-dam committee was made into a prominent feature story, complete with a picture of the mayor helping a pretty woman into a plastic swimming pool, which supposedly represented "Blue Lake." The masthead on the Sunday comics, meanwhile, underwent a sudden change from plain block lettering to an elaborate banner picturing an idyllic blue lake bordered by green rolling hills and peopled with hunters, fishermen, boaters, and a pretty blond water-skier. Such a scene did not then exist in Humboldt County; where else could it be but in visionary Butler Valley?

Despite support from the newspaper and the powers-that-be, Butler Valley Dam went down to a resounding two-to-one defeat. Proponents of the dam, including the land speculators whose plans for developing the area had failed, were puzzled. What had gone wrong?

The time used to be that if Uncle Sam offered to build you a dam and pick up half the tab, you'd gladly accept. Those were the days before Environmental Impact Statements and small taxpayers' revolts, when "bigger" meant "better" and happiness was measured in numbers. When a group of powerful Eureka businessmen proposed the construction of Ruth Dam in the 1950's, they met with little organized opposition and the required bond issue passed easily by a 69 percent vote. Even in 1969, when congressional action paved the way for the Butler Valley Dam, the local newspaper simply *assumed* that the dam would come to pass: "An eleven-mile-long lake on the Mad River just a half-hour drive from Eureka, new industry and more shipping on Humboldt Bay, adequate water for city growth—these are the advances coming in the mid-1970's because of favorable congressional action Tuesday on Butler Valley Dam and the bay improvement project." Then, when a woman named Donna Henkins told a few of her friends, "You know, I think we can stop Butler Valley," they thought she was crazy. Nobody could stand in the way of a federally financed dam.

But something has changed in the last few years. Dam proposals are still a dime a dozen, yet the dams themselves are harder to come by now. "This kind of thing is nothing new around here," says a long-time resident of the county. "It's been going on for twenty-five years. But now the people won't go for it any more." Partly, the change has been due to an increasing conservatism concerning governmental expenditures of any sort. But the change has also been due to a heightened environmental consciousness and to new laws which reflect that consciousness. Before they could go ahead and dam up Butler Valley, the Army Corps of Engineers now had to submit an Environmental Impact Statement, which, by its very nature, was bound to raise serious questions about the validity of the project:

Approximately 2,360 acres of one of the few remaining non-urbanized, sparsely populated fertile valleys in northern California and about nine miles of free-flowing river will be covered by the reservoir waters. The area is scarcely used by man at the present time, so that noise and other pollution levels in the area are insignificant. The type of outdoor experience in this relatively scenic river area is not unique, but the availability of similar areas is limited.

Numerous species of terrestrial and avian wildlife, which depend on the valley environment and the relative seclusion of the area, will be displaced and eventually will die. The existing wildlife in the area will be replaced by species which are more suited to a reservoir environment. However, these species will be limited in number because of the close proximity to man, the fluctuating characteristics of the reservoir waters, and the lack of lakeside shallow areas.

The species of living organisms which inhabit a still-lake environment are indeed quite different from those which inhabit the waters and banks of fast-moving streams. And so it is with human cultures. Diverse and isolated springs and streams lend themselves to decentralized living arrangements: small farms and homesteads sporadically situated off in the backcountry, each utilizing the water from its own nearby source. Large lakes and reservoirs, on the other hand, tend to concentrate people as well as water in a central location: no city can exist without a sizable water source to service its inhabitants. But lakes also tend to centralize the recreational use of the countryside. Hikers and hunters spread themselves out into the woods, but boaters and water-skiers, of necessity, must share a common space. Consequently, lakes are obvious sites for recreationally oriented development, for they concentrate large numbers of people in relatively small areas. "This place is really ripe," remarked a real estate man who was passing through the Whitethorn area in search of opportunities for investment. "All it needs is a large body of standing water."

But lakes do not form naturally in this hilly terrain where all water rushes quickly into the Pacific Ocean nearby. If you want a lake, you have to build one yourself. So, taking little notice of the pre-existing countryside, along come the engineers who propose to re-create the world after their own image. "If lakes are what you want," they say, "then we have the know-how to build them."

The engineers, however, are more than just pawns in the service of powerful businessmen and entrepreneurs. Their job is to build dams, and without dams to build they would be unemployed. Philip Starr, who spent several months dealing with the proponents of the Whitethorn Dam, sums up what he learned about the engineers' world:

"The Department of Water Resources just follows Parkinson's Law: you know, there's a bureaucracy there, and they build dams. They're predisposed by who they are, and by their talents, to build dams. And when they run out of dams on big rivers, then they'll start looking for other places to dam. That's what they did here. The Mattole was going to be their pilot study, so then they could do it to *all* of the North Coast rivers. Fix them all, see, because they've all been ruined by logging. Every single one, all of them are in line for that as a 'restoration process' rather than dealing with the basic problem: that the watershed is ruined. Instead of doing something about the watershed itself in its natural state, you do some other man-made thing. Because that's the idea we have of what people are to be employed doing: human beings are to employ themselves in *changing* everything, as if somehow it isn't right the way it is.

"So here's Barnes and Dolcini [Ed Barnes's boss at the D.W.R.], both living up in Red Bluff, and they've run out of rivers and they're both aching for the Mattole, and here I happen to live under where they want to put their dam. And every time I go down the valley, *I* see water a hundred feet overhead and condominiums on the shores, and *they* see employment for themselves and for the people that work for them, and great loads of fun, because that's what they do: they build dams, that's their identity, it's the connection they have with things."

There is something patently absurd about these governmental agencies proposing to construct two dams at the same time: one geared specifically to counter the depopulation of salmon and steelhead trout, and another that would kill off thousands of those very same fish. The rationalized manipulation of the environment has obviously become somewhat *irrational* when such an obvious contradiction is never even questioned by the bureaucracies involved. If it seems absurd to construct a multimillion-dollar concrete wall in order to trade off trees, wildlife, and people for (possibly) a few fish, it is equally absurd to spend a hundred thousand dollars (for that was Ed Barnes's budget) just to consider such a scheme. If it seems absurd to trade off an "endangered species" of small homesteaders and ranchers for a playground for the well-to-do, it is equally absurd for one group of people who have no connection at all with the land to impose their will on the local inhabitants—human and nonhuman alike.

True, neither dam is being built—at least for the time being. It is a tribute to the reason and power of the common people that dams are no longer simplistically equated with Progress and the General Good. Yet the forces which gave rise to the Butler Valley and Whitethorn project proposals are still very much alive—government agencies whose business it is to build dams, real estate speculators and developers, economic interests which threaten to transform the shape and texture of the countryside. The battle of the Edges continues as the available space on earth contracts day by day. There are only so many rivers to be dammed, or not to be dammed, as the case may be.

A dam, indeed, is a "psychological symbol"—not only of economic growth but also of technological power. To build a mountain in the middle of a river—what a monumental demonstration of man's ability to manipulate the environment to suit his fancy! But when a dam gets stopped before it is ever built— that too is a "psychological symbol" for those who would like to see some check to the destructive transformation of the natural world and to the rapid development and commercialization of the backcountry. The conservationists' victory, however, is in a sense a hollow one: what we are left with is only what was there in the first place. Our energy has been expended not in seeking out positive ways of relating to our world, but in fighting the negative forces which threaten it. After all is said and done, the salmon and steelhead populations on the Mattole are still declining, and the economy of Humboldt County remains depressed. The proposed dams were obviously only pseudo-solutions—yet that is not to deny the reality of the problems they were supposed to solve.

Part Six
POSSIBILITIES

Only thing left for this country around here
is when they strike oil. . . .
Who knows what's gonna happen next?

—AN OLD-TIMER

———————————————

15

In This Day and Age

THE CRUSH IS ON. If only by reason of our mushrooming population, the American countryside can no longer expect to be protected by isolation from the rest of the modern world. The people of the Metropolis must be fed, and they must have somewhere to go as a temporary escape from the hectic pace of city life. For better or for worse recreational land has assumed equal importance with farm land in the minds of the urbanites. The country folk, however, would have it otherwise: the dams, parks, freeways, and second-home developments signal an end to their domination of the forests and fields they would like to call home. Yet the country folk are few, the city folk many. So the question inevitably arises: Is the exclusive enjoyment of the countryside by the people who live there a luxury we can no longer afford? Is the preservation of country culture worth the price, in the form of land, we would have to pay? Now that our space on earth appears so limited, how can we determine whose needs should first be met?

Recently I had occasion to spend two months in the city of San Francisco. Being a lover of the outdoors, I naturally joined the throngs of city dwellers who flock to the surrounding countryside at every available opportunity. On one three-day weekend in the middle of February, I found myself driving back from the Santa Cruz Mountains by way of the San Francisco Peninsula. The alternating meadows and forests on either side of the narrow road were an inviting sight, yet I was inhibited in my desire to get out of the car and stretch my legs by a never-ending stream of barbed-wire fences. Finally there was a gap in the fencing; I pulled off the road near a long-neglected orchard and started to climb an adjacent hill which showed no signs of human habitation.

"Hey, dude, you can't go up there," said a voice from out of nowhere. I turned around, and sure enough the man was addressing himself to me. "I'm sorry, but it's private property, you know." I wanted to assure him that I would set no fires and leave no beer cans, but how could he possibly distinguish me from less responsible visitors? How could he tell one stranger from the next? And besides, I thought to myself, the man is entitled to his privacy.

The fences continued, mile after mile. Sometimes they were necessary to contain the livestock within, but much of the land was forested and the fences there seemed to be geared primarily toward keeping the roadside visitors out. At the next break in the fencing there was a discreet wooden sign: "Sunnyvale Mountain Park." I pulled in, only to discover that I would have to pay a fee of a quarter if I simply wished to get out of my car. I hesitated, not because the price was exorbitant but because I just wasn't sure I wanted to pay for a walk in the woods. One's experience in a park, furthermore, tends to be charted out in advance, while I prefer a little bit of adventure, a touch of the unexpected. Philosophical objections aside, however, it was worth a quarter just to stretch my legs. I got out of my car and ventured forth toward the solitary figure who functioned as a gatekeeper.

"Where should I park?" I asked him.

"Are you a resident of Sunnyvale?" he asked in return.

"No, just passing through."

"I'm sorry, but this park is only for Sunnyvale residents and their invited guests," he told me. Alas, I couldn't even *buy* my way out of my car and into the woods.

Several miles farther on there was another break in the fence. This time a dozen cars were parked by the side of the road, and an occasional group of people could be seen wandering over the nearby hillsides. I asked a teen-age boy who was standing by his car whether this was a public place.

"This is Aquarian Valley," he told me.

"Is it a park, or who owns it?"

"I dunno who owns it, but we've been coming here for years."

"So I can just walk around and nobody will kick me off?"

"Sure. Everybody comes just to get loose and stay high. You know, party. There's a waterfall down below."

I wasn't exactly up for a party, but at least I could take a walk and refresh myself before returning to the city for another week. I started off across a field toward the west. I wasn't gone for more than five minutes, however, when a blue-and-white helicopter buzzed over my head and an ominous voice came from out of the sky: "This is the Sheriff's Office. You are trespassing on private property. If you do not leave this area you will be subject to arrest and your car will be towed away." The helicopter circled around, repeating its message four or five times, and then disappeared over the eastern horizon.

Now, I'm not generally obsessed with paranoia, but I did feel that the cards were definitely stacked against me just then. All I wanted was a brief walk in the open air. To either side of the road I could see miles and miles of uninhabited countryside, yet I was denied any access to it. I found myself, quite literally, on the other side of the fence: no longer was I a rural resident protecting the integrity of the land around me from fun-seeking tourists; instead, I was temporarily in the position of the city dwellers who want, or even need, a little room in which to breathe. The desire of city folk for outdoor recreation is very real indeed—even if it does pose a threat to the people and places of the Edges.

Despite the ubiquitous barbed-wire fences, many country people are quite hospitable to visitors who are willing to pay for their amusements. Throughout much of the countryside, tourism has become a major industry. The urbanites who come to the California North with money to spend are seen as a potential salvation for its lumber-depleted and overgrazed economy. An economy geared toward recreation, however, means subdivisions like Shelter Cove, freeways like those which bisected Frank Nervo's vineyard, and dams like those proposed for

Whitethorn and Butler Valley. It means that water-skiing and motorboating, standardized American images of outdoor recreation, will take the place of more private, decentralized amusements. It means that land—woods and meadows, hills and valleys —will be thought of in terms of "acreage" and "parcels." It means that the engineers—road builders, dam builders, and developers—will be given the go-ahead to transform the countryside into what it is not. And, in the final analysis, it means an end to rural, independent lifestyles; it means that the Edges will be subsumed by the Metropolis.

How can the Edges be preserved in the face of such pressures? The forces of history cannot be altered by simply wishing them away. There are strong—and real—reasons for the modernized development of the countryside. As a social critic, I can't help but feel frustration at not being able to personally ensure the preservation of country culture. But there isn't that much a single individual can do about it, and even people in positions of power are relatively helpless in the face of social and cultural forces which are so large, yet so nebulous, as "modernization." As the old saying goes, " "You can't legislate morality." There is no way we can enforce an appreciation of rodeos and county fairs, nor can we dictate that ranches and small towns should not be allowed to change with the times.

We can, however, deal with some of the more manageable issues in the realm of politics and economics. Governmental policies such as building codes and taxation measures have a marked effect on the fate of the countryside, while economic necessity plays a major role in shaping both landscape and lifestyle along the Edges. It is in the name of economic development that the Edges are being consumed, and it is bureaucratic pressure applied by governmental agencies which is hastening the downfall of individualized, self-sufficient country living.

The solution to the problem of bureaucracy is obvious: loosen up the various restrictions to a point where they are back in harmony with the needs and realities of rural living. If this requires separate laws for the city and the country, that is a technical rather than a philosophical consideration. Waste disposal for an apartment building, for instance, is an altogether different matter from what it is for a mountain cabin, and there is no reason why our laws cannot be flexible enough to take heed of that difference.

The problem of economic development, however, is more complicated. The backcountry is indeed impoverished, for its resources have been depleted and not restored. It hungers for economic activity, but such activity only tends to deplete its resources even further and to mar its landscapes. It is thus caught in a vicious circle: it is confronted with the paradoxical choice between modernization and development on the one hand and preservation of the land—but also economic impoverishment—on the other. The Edges don't particularly wish to be subsumed by the Metropolis, but neither do they wish to remain jobless by leaving everything the way it is. Economics or ecology—which way will it go?

There are in fact alternative resolutions to the apparent dilemma. The dichotomy between economics and ecology is based on the false assumption that the needs of man are inherently contradictory to those of nonhuman life forms. It is incorrect to conclude that man must always make his living in an exploitive manner simply because he has tended to do so in the recent past. In place of this pessimistic analysis I would offer a more positive premise: man is a part of the environment. With this basic idea in mind, we can look toward methods of "development" which cater to the needs of man and nature alike, which provide jobs for humans while simultaneously enabling nonhuman species to flourish.

There are three simple guidelines which I feel should be applied to any development program intended for the economic and ecological benefit of the countryside. First, it should have the net effect of increasing rather than exhausting the natural resources of the earth as a whole. Second, it should pump money directly into the local economy whenever and wherever possible, thus relieving some of the economic pressures which further exploit the land. And third, it should help to promote self-supporting economic endeavors which utilize the truly renewable resources of the local landscape.

Dams, freeways, and second-home developments fail on all

three counts. In the first place, dams and freeways require mountain upon mountain of concrete and untold quantities of fuel to run the massive, earth-moving equipment; thus they contribute to the further depletion of the world's precious resources. Second-home communities, on their part, use up more than their share of wood for houses which are only partially utilized. Secondly, most of the work on such large-scale operations is generally done by high-priced engineers and construction workers called in for the job—not by the folks of the Edges, the ones who still live on the land. And finally, the most significant economic impact of dams, freeways, and second-home developments is limited to the period of construction. After the work is done, the only local industry that stands to benefit from these massive capital expenditures is tourism, an industry of personal service to people from afar. Of all the possible economic endeavors for the people of the countryside, tourism is least suited to sustained self-sufficiency.

What other possibilities for development are there? Each specific community has to look toward alternatives which best fit in with its natural potential. As an example of how these simple criteria might be beneficially applied to local situations, I will offer here some suggestions for my own particular Edges— the backcountry of northern California, where forestry, fishing, and agriculture presently constitute the basis for the human economy.

FORESTRY

Most of our virgin timber has long since vanished. Even the stubborn holdouts who tried to preserve their forests have for the most part succumbed under the pressure of being taxed anew on the full market value of their trees every year. But what has become of the logged-over land? Few of the owners have seen fit to become involved in the process of forest restoration, since any rewards for their efforts would not be realized for at least half a century. From our individualistic perspective, such a long-term investment hardly seems worthwhile. No one knows what history has in store, and there is no guarantee that reforested

land will not be usurped for other uses at some point within the
next fifty or one hundred years.

Public agencies should have been more attuned to long-term
perspectives, but only recently has the government taken any
interest at all. Under the Forestry Incentives Program created in
1973, small landowners can now receive some assistance in replanting, thinning, and pruning their youthful forests. This is
certainly a step in the right direction. Forests in their natural
state are not accustomed to the kind of devastation caused by
logging operations, and they could certainly use some assistance
in staging a comeback. In addition to replanting trees, altering
the drainage along the old skid roads would help prevent erosion
and the logging debris could be removed from the stream beds
below. What would be the cost of this type of program? For the
price of a single dam, the entire watershed of the affected river
could be made almost as good as new—and the money would
stretch much further, for reforestation, unlike dam building, is
decentralized work requiring a minimum of heavy equipment
and a maximum of manpower. The money would fall into the
hands of the people of the Edges instead of being used up in
wearing out the machines.

The main objective of reforestation, however, is not simply
to create employment. We have exhausted the productivity of
our forests by cutting them down at a faster rate than they can
grow back. The backcountry—trees and people alike—has been
exploited by the omniverous appetite of a consumption-oriented
society. The problem now is to get the countryside back on its
feet, to establish a program of sustained yield in which the harvest does not exceed the growth.

FISHING

The quick and easy way of expanding the fishing industry
would be to put more boats in the ocean, and thereby to catch
more fish. But this method would be short-lived, for the problem faced by commercial fishermen does not lie in the number of
their boats but rather in the number of fish in the ocean. Since
the anadromous salmon and steelhead trout depend on fresh

water as well as sea water to live, they have been adversely affected by poor watershed management. The wholesale destruction of the coastal forests in the past thirty years has covered their gravel spawning beds with silt, smothered their eggs, and hindered their migration by jamming the streams with debris. The result has been the reduction of the salmon and steelhead populations which use the north coastal streams to one third their former size.

How could we help the fish stage a comeback—and thereby help ourselves? We could, of course, spend tens of millions of dollars to place "experimental" dams on the rivers (as, for example, the proposed Whitethorn Dam) to see if that might help—but dams have hitherto been a major part of the problem, and it is unreasonable to expect that they would suddenly become the solution. We could develop more and better fish hatcheries—but these are delicate and sensitive operations, and thousands of fish can be lost at a single shot if everything is not just right. Or we could go right to the cause of the problem: the watersheds themselves. If the forests were somehow restored, the fish, over a period of time, might do the rest of the job on their own. The same reforestation projects intended to revitalize timber production would thus also add to the renewable resources of our waterways—and consequently of the ocean. They would provide short-term employment for workers in the woods and long-term employment for the fishermen themselves.

AGRICULTURE

In 1970 there were only half as many farms in California as there were twenty-five years earlier. During that period, however, the size of the average farm doubled and the value of the average farm increased tenfold due to skyrocketing land values and food prices. As agribusiness has taken over the land, the relative importance of the farmers themselves has dwindled to next to nothing. In 1940 the farm population accounted for almost 10 percent of the people in California; by 1970 the farmers and their families amounted to less than 1 percent of the state's total

—even though California is the number-one agricultural state in the nation.

On one level the modern plantations which have come to dominate the agricultural landscape appear to have made food production more efficient. But such efficiency is not without its hidden costs. Complicated, fuel-consuming machinery is needed to harvest the crops, while additional fuel and machinery are needed to transport them from one end of the country to the other. Production depends on high-cost fertilizers which are not recycled and pesticides which in many cases *are* recycled. Single-crop farming, furthermore, has eliminated many natural protections against pests and diseases, thus requiring a further dependence upon stronger and stronger pesticides which are necessary to cope with new strains of the crops' enemies. We have yet to see the final results of this vicious circle, but if we project the trend of the past twenty-five years forward for a century or two, the consequences appear rather frightening indeed.

Small, decentralized farming is perhaps less efficient, but it does escape many of the portentous hazards of agribusiness. A well-balanced farm is less susceptible to total devastation by insects or diseases, and the dependence on pesticides is consequently diminished. Animal wastes can be utilized for building up the soil, thus minimizing the need for importing fertilizers from elsewhere. Fuel consumption can be lessened by doing some of the work by hand, while transportation costs need not be so great since the markets would generally be closer to home. And then there are the people themselves: more folks can be gainfully employed directly in the food-producing process, and more food can be consumed which never goes through the market.

I don't mean to suggest by these observations that all large, single-crop farms should automatically be divided and sold, but rather that smaller, diversified farms have much to recommend them and should not be mercilessly eliminated from the countryside in the name of mechanical efficiency. Particularly in backhill areas such as my own, the small, diversified farm is perhaps the most logical way to utilize the growing potential of the land. In the past decade the percentage of California farms under ten acres has suddenly taken an upswing, and it seems unlikely that the interest in small-scale farming is simply a passing fad. With both land and food becoming precious commodities, more and more people are showing an eagerness to claim and grow their own.

Partly, the government seems responsive to the needs of these would-be farmers. Advisers are ready and willing to help, while there are a host of cost-sharing programs designed to facilitate the transformation of land into agricultural pursuits. But then there are other government agencies that are often aligned against the small-time agrarian entrepreneurs. Health inspectors issue strict regulations against selling home-butchered meat or home-grown milk, while the planners and building inspectors keep a close and inhibiting eye on everything from human habitations to chicken coops. Irrigation districts blatantly ignore Reclamation Act provisions which forbid absentee owners or large-scale holdings, preferring instead to let the companies and conglomerates reap the full benefits from federally financed projects. And the very same government which would reclaim the desert for farm land also endeavors to eliminate farming from the fertile, silt-laden flood plains by means of expensive "flood control" projects which would "secure" the regions for commerce and industry.

NATIVE FOODS

Agriculture can become addicting. Our society is so focused on food *production* that it totally ignores food sources that grow naturally all around us: acorns, cattails, pine nuts, berries, and so on. Acorns, for instance, constituted the staple food of the California Indians. Acorn mush, acorn bread, or pemmican—scarcely a meal ever lacked the presence of the fruits from the oak trees. The Indians of northwestern California (from the Mendocino-Sonoma line to the Oregon border) harvested approximately five million pounds of acorns a year—enough to supply our modern-day population of the same area with well over a hundred pounds of acorns for every family. Most of the oak trees are still with us, and the acorns are just as nutritious now as they were then: approximately 20 percent fat, 5 percent protein, and 60 percent carbohydrate, with traces of calcium, magnesium, phosphorus, potassium, and sulfur. Why, then, are the acorns so totally neglected today?

Primitive peoples in the Old World utilized acorns, but when the Europeans turned toward agriculture they found it possible to meet their cereal needs with other foods while simultaneously using the acorns to fatten their hogs. From there on out, acorns were loaded with pejorative connotations: "primitive," "peasant," "starvation food"—and "pigs." According to the sixteenth-century English herbalist John Gerrard: "Acorns, if they be eaten are hardly concocted, they yield no nourishment to man's body, but that which is grosse, raw, and cold. Swine are fatted herewith, and by feeding thereon have their flesh hard and sound." When the white settlers in California found the countryside covered with oak trees, they consequently never even thought of eating the acorns themselves; instead, they turned loose their pigs to forage in the woods.

If we wanted to reclaim the life-supporting acorns for human consumption today, we would have to start "farming" the forests as the Indians once did: we'd have to burn off the first-fallen, worm-infested acorns for a year or two to get the oak moth population back under control. But even with the oak "orchards" back in shape, we'd have the problem of educating the public to a totally unfamiliar food item. It is unreasonable to expect private capital to be expended in such an unorthodox and speculative endeavor, but it would not be unreasonable at all for our government to put a tiny portion of its extensive resources into an experimental program which might, in the long run, make a significant contribution to the country's food sources. Through modern research techniques, new varieties of trees or higher yields from the old ones might be attained. Perhaps the oak tree is the ideal tool to convert nature's energy into human food in rugged areas of the backcountry where other forms of farming are not feasible.

The oaks, furthermore, aren't the only neglected wild food. The ridgetops of the California North are covered with manzanita bushes, which in turn are covered with bright red berries that the settlers, for some reason, assumed to be poisonous. Yet manzanita berries furnished the Indians with all the vitamin C they could ever use; indeed, they are far more potent than oranges in this respect. And they are easy to gather, too: several pounds will fall to the ground from a single bush if you simply shake the branches. Again, however, problems of consumer education and marketing make it difficult for private citizens to become involved in such a project. Yet if some groundwork were laid, the California backcountry might have a few more jobs and the earth a new supply of food.

Here it is acorns and manzanita berries; elsewhere, there are pine nuts, mesquite beans, cattails, and a host of other wild foods which once nourished the hunting-and-gathering populations of North America. Throughout the countryside there are neglected food sources which have been overlooked primarily because we did not plant them ourselves. True, wild foods do not generally produce as heavy a yield per acre as domesticated foods; the food, however, is already *there*—and it is not being used.

Aside from their availability, crops such as acorns bear the advantage of constituting an easily renewable resource which is certainly compatible with other uses of the same land. Such is not the case with many of our natural resources. The present prognosis for the California oak forests, for instance, is to turn them into wood chips and thence into paper products; once the forests are gone, the boom will be followed by yet another bust. Harvesting the acorns, on the other hand, would leave the forests intact (many oaks don't even use the acorns for purposes of reproduction, propagating themselves vegetatively instead). The choice between wood chips and acorns is a choice between exhaustive or sustained utilization of natural resources.

Whether "development" of the backcountry comes in the form of reforestation, watershed improvement, reclaiming marginal farm land, or the harvesting of native foods, the returns from any investment are likely to be gradual and diffuse rather than quick and specific. Private individuals or companies are likely to shy away from investments which will take twenty, fifty, or a hundred years to turn a profit. In the case of watershed improvement, no private interest can be expected to spend all that money and energy for the long-term benefit of the fish which they have no guarantee of catching themselves. Insofar as development requires capital, the most logical organizations to undertake the task would seem to lie in the governmental sector.

Yet governmental involvement inevitably involves bureaucracies and regulations which can easily get out of step with the needs of private citizens. The people of the Edges already have enough problems with technical legalities which seem to have a will of their own. How can I possibly advocate governmental action when so many of the problems I have recorded in the previous pages are due to the intrusion of governmental bodies into private affairs?

In fact, I am not advocating an *increase* in governmental involvement in the development of the countryside. The government is *already* involved, whether we like it or not. It builds freeways and dams, lays out parks and irrigation canals, taxes land and timber, and regulates all construction activities as well as the marketing of food. It proposed to spend twelve million dollars on the Whitethorn Dam and seven times that much on the Butler Valley project. Governmental expenditures are indicators of social priorities, and it is those priorities that must be changed. It is thus not the size of the expenditures that is being questioned so much as the choice of projects which would be of greatest service to the land and the people of the backcountry. We don't need dams, we don't need make-work handouts—but we do need to get our resources back into an equilibrium which is supportive of human life on a long-range basis.

Even if done correctly, large-scale expenditures on ecologically oriented projects would not constitute a cure-all for our problems. Our lives out here on the Edges are by nature and geography somewhat isolated; our means of livelihood would consequently do best to reflect rather than subvert our tendency toward decentralization. By providing for many of our own needs on an individual basis, we solidify our own economic position while simultaneously removing our names from the list of those who must be cared for by industry, agribusiness, and other centralized means of production. Indeed, large-scale problems such as food and fuel shortages are generally tackled only with large-scale solutions such as corporate farming and atomic-energy plants; rarely do we bother to investigate how decentralized methods might be used to solve those very same problems. Yet marginal farming and the harnessing of wind and solar energy might go a long way toward fulfilling the food and fuel needs of those with access to even minimal plots of land, thus relieving some of the pressure created by other segments of an overdemanding, overconsuming society.

It is generally assumed by engineers and laymen alike that the efficiency of any operation increases with size. But this does not always hold true. The per capita cost of food distribution and waste disposal, for instance, is less in a medium-sized town than in a large city. Likewise, the food yield from a series of small, diversified farms might be more than that of a large ranch which, in the interests of labor-saving economy, permits only cattle to graze on the land. With the imminent exhaustion of the world's supply of fossil fuel, the question of centralization is bound to come to a head: will we turn toward the intensely concentrated form of energy found within the atom, an energy which can only be extracted with much technological apparatus in a handful of well-equipped locations, or will we instead turn toward the more diffuse energy of the sun and the wind, an energy which can be harnessed in bits and pieces by small-scale operations scattered throughout the land?

On a strictly personal level, I lean toward decentralized solutions whenever they appear feasible. Perhaps an insidious country conservatism has crept into my blood, for I am fearful of the enforced standardization which tends to accompany centralized institutions. One of the major arguments for preserving the agrarian culture of the people of the Edges is based on the need for maintaining diversity: the country culture still exists, if only tenuously; we would be doing us all a disservice were we to wipe it from the face of the earth. If people have strong familial ties, by all means let them remain with their families; if people have roots in the land, do not force them from their homes; if people want to raise their own food and build their own shelters, there is no reason to deny them their will. The people of the Edges, in short, are engaged in a perfectly viable way of life which represents an alternative to metropolitan lifestyles; to centralize all production and all decisions would necessarily constitute an added threat to the continued existence of the alternatives offered on the Edges.

Finally, we ought to remember that no single development— nor even any single program for development—constitutes a solution to the social, economic, and ecological problems faced by the countryside. We must come down off our grand solutions, however susceptible we may be to the seductive appeal of our own rhetoric. I may present some suggestions, but I can hardly pretend to know all the answers for the people and places of the Edges. At best, what I have offered in these pages is an attitude, a method of analysis: for each situation we encounter, we ought to consider the needs of city folk and country folk alike, as well as the needs of other life forms; we ought to keep an eye to the traditions of the past, while realizing that the future is bound to be different; we ought to recognize that particular people and places of the Edges embody a uniqueness, an individuality, which is worthy of being preserved. And above all, we ought never to forget that human beings are part of the environment. Any violence we inflict on the world reflects back upon us, yet as living creatures on earth we owe it to ourselves to secure a respectable niche in the overall scheme of things.

A Note on the Type

This book was set on the Linotype in Janson, a recutting made direct from type cast from matrices long thought to have been made by the Dutchman Anton Janson, who was a practicing type founder in Leipzig during the years 1668–87. However, it has been conclusively demonstrated that these types are actually the work of Nicholas Kis (1650–1702), a Hungarian, who most probably learned his trade from the master Dutch type founder Dirk Voskens. The type is an excellent example of the influential and sturdy Dutch types that prevailed in England up to the time William Caslon developed his own incomparable designs from them.

Composed, printed, and bound by
American Book–Stratford Press, Inc.,
Saddle Brook, New Jersey.

Designed by Gwen Townsend